Heavy Metal

A Tribute to Manholes

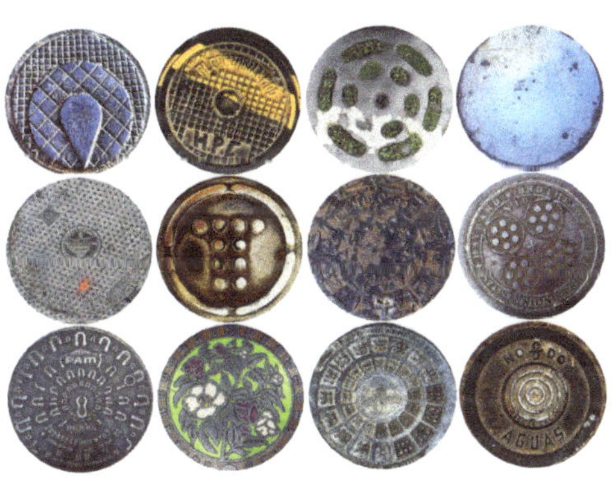

Peter Sishton

Published in 2023

by FunkistKunst

ISBN: 978-1-913898-49-6

Cover and Book interior Design by Russell Holden
www.pixeltweakspublications.com

“We are all in the gutter
but some of us are looking at the manholes”

Sarah Abdullala

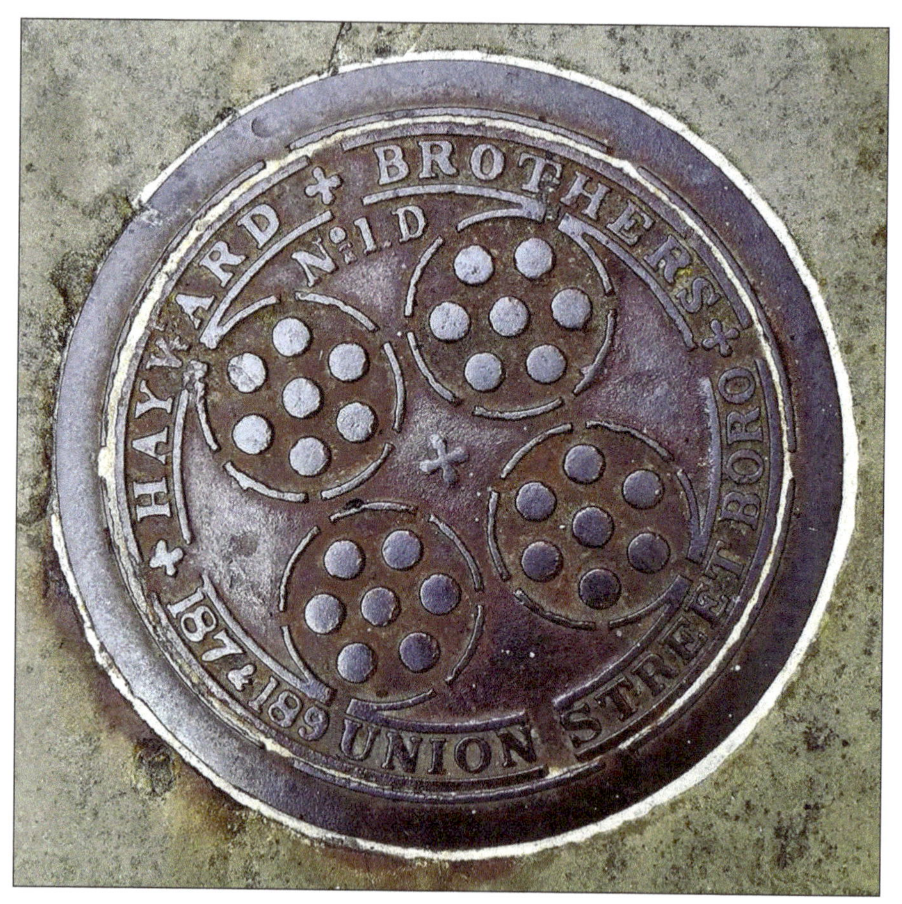
HAYWARD + BROTHERS +
No. 1.D
1874 189 UNION STREET BORO

Heavy Metal A Tribute to Manholes is dedicated to my mum and dad, my brother Steve, my daughters Molly and Connie, and granddaughter Olivia, not to forget Sir Stanley Whippet.

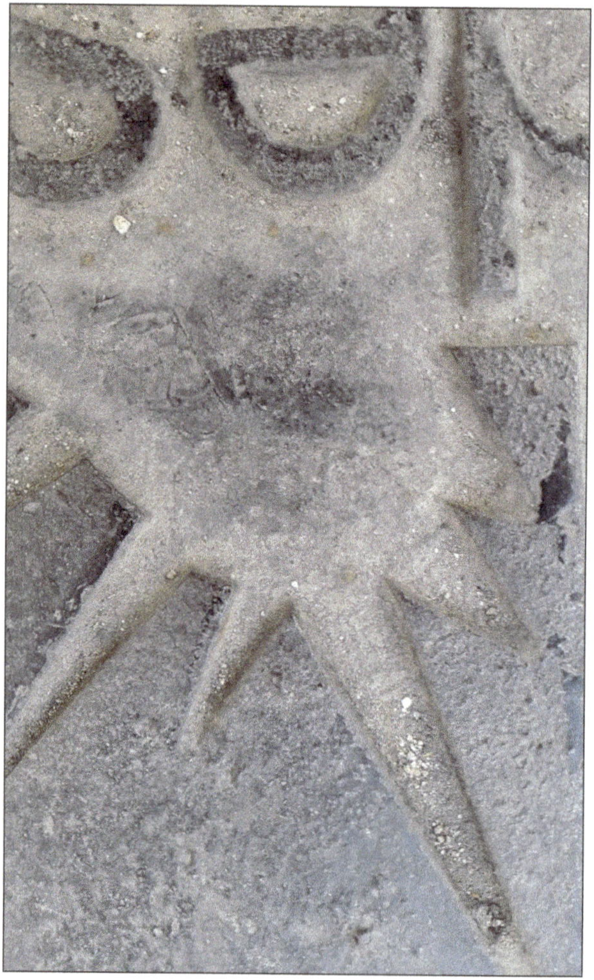

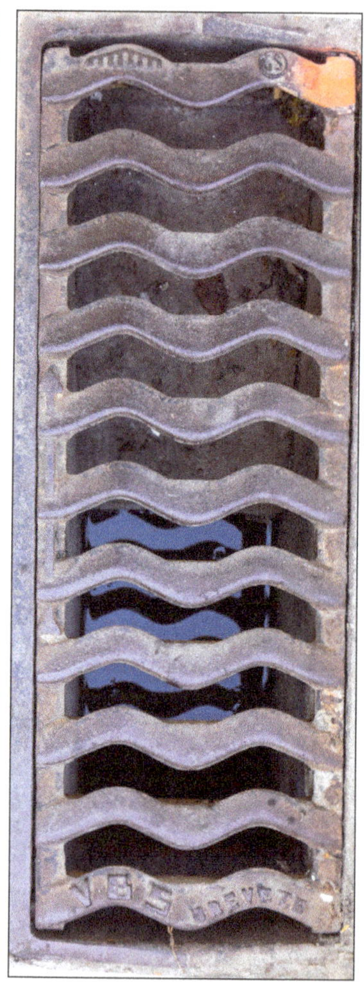
VBS

Contents

Why are manholes around?

A poetical reflection of Peter Sishton by Ali Gadema, courtesy of John Mgrath and Ali Gadema as part of Manchester International Festival 2021

Hey, look at that manhole cover that's a really fine manhole cover someone took their time designing that manhole cover good job it's not a square manhole cover don't want a hole without a manhole cover check out that manhole cover that's a museum piece manhole cover Thomas Crapper designed that manhole cover fuuucking hell what a manhole cover that's Jeremy Corbyn's manhole cover that's one boring arse manhole cover wow that's an intricate manhole cover yeah its a Japanese manhole cover they're deadly serious about manhole covers Jennifer L Knox couldn't even write that manhole cover I dread to think what's underneath that manhole cover actually there's some pretty intricate engineering beneath that manhole cover people fall in love over manhole covers I wanna flip that lid and roll that manhole cover down the road and back line it up replace it and walk all over that manhole cover better yet I wanna wear that manhole cover better yet I wanna wear that manhole cover like a ruff in a mediaeval court I'd be Peter the Great of manhole covers with a manhole cover crown.

What's that?

Oh.

I'm supposed to call them personnel hole covers.

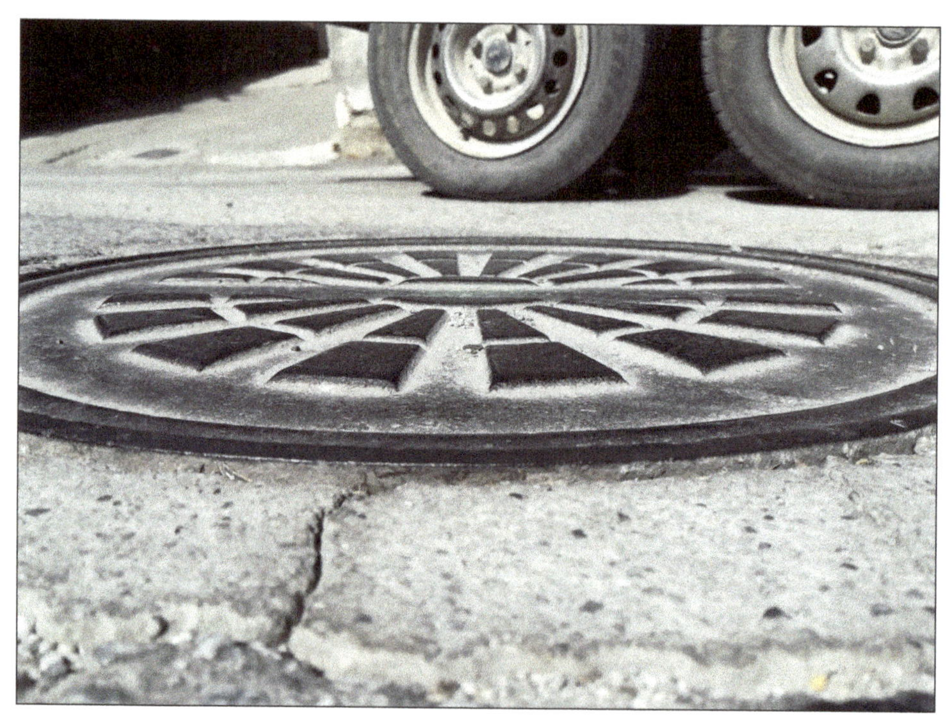

Acknowledgements

Molly and Connie Sishton and Georgia

Hilary Spronken

Alan Bloomfield and Bryan Robert Bale

Mel and James

Sue Densley

Zarah Abdullala

Phil Hall

John Magrath and Ali Gadema Manchester International Festival

My heartfelt thanks to the wonderful people above. Molly and Connie Sishton for supporting me throughout the artistic process, from conception to my first exhibition. Also for encouraging me to develop the manhole project over the last few years, and helping with the construction and design of the FunkistKunst website, the portal to all of the manhole images that are for sale. Lastly, for being the best daughters in the world.

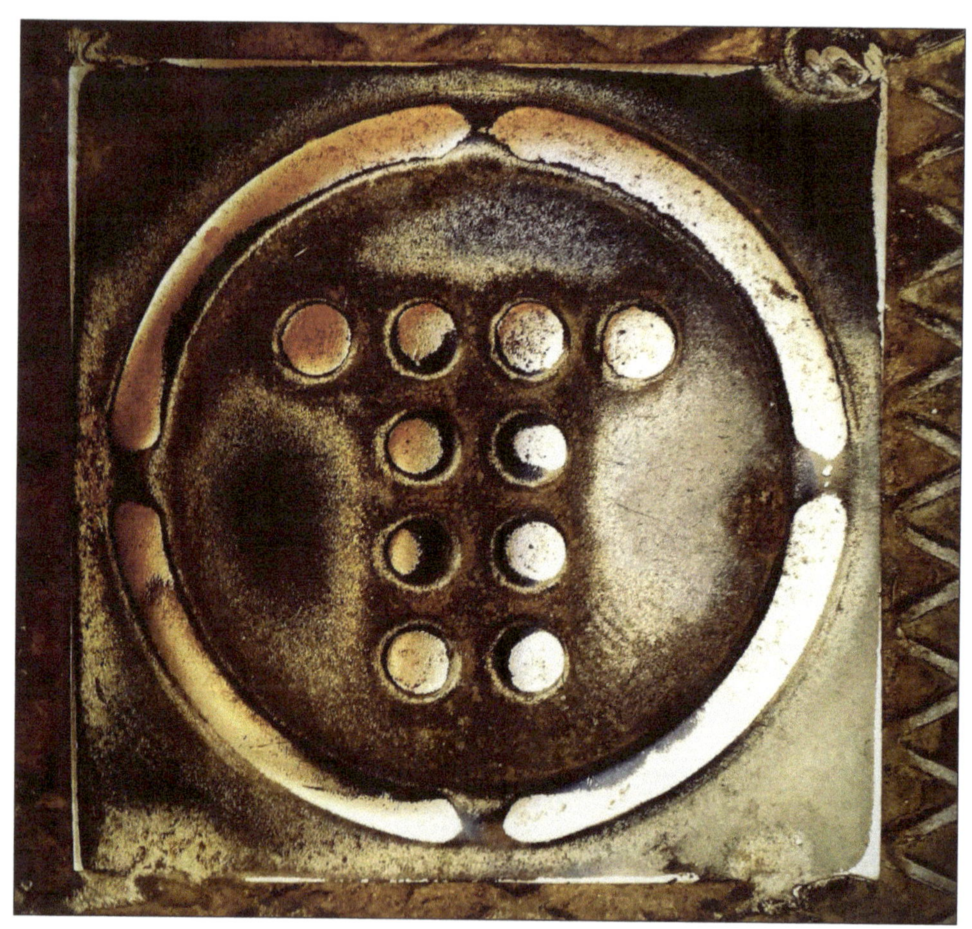

XII

Very special thanks to four of my dearest friends Hilary Spronken, Sarah Frances, Phil Hall and Alan Bloomfield for their invaluable editing skills and help in completing the book.

Great thanks to the late Bryan Robert Bale for his artistic support and Alan Bloomfield for his invaluable direction with post production processing without which none of this would have been possible and for contributing a couple of superb images.

Also a big thank you to Sue Densley who kindly took time on her trip to seek out a Matsuyama manhole. One of which is included in this book. Not least a huge thank you to all my friends who helped with my Gofundme contributions.

Foreword

Keeping something covered, out of site, away from view, putting the lid on it, closing lid... Every single survivor has their own unique way of healing, of expressing themselves in using creativity to say something about the unsaid. I have always admired survivors journeys, artists expressions, and the creation of something new that you get to see through their eyes.

Thank you to every survivor for inspiring me. Thank you to every artist, dancer, performer, musician, singer, song writer, author, poet, painter, sculptur, and photographer for giving me insight.

From covering and being shut out or in the dark, to the uncovering flow of light that besets the tunnel will be a journey many understand but not many voice.

Healing is a journey and not a destination.

Duncan Craig OBE

Chief Executive Officer, Survivors Manchester

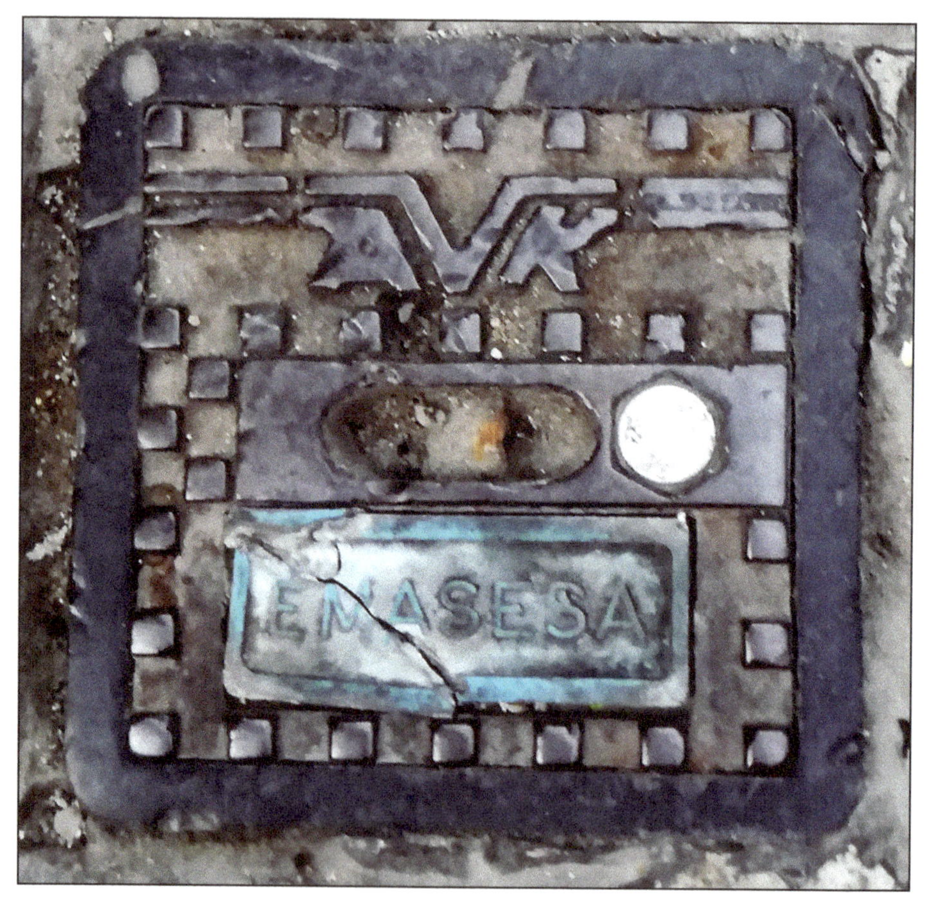
EMASESA

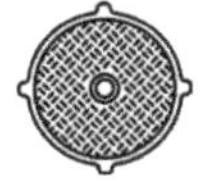

Introduction

My interest in manholes came about during the summer of 2016 on a visit to St-Jean-d'Angely, in the Charente-Maritime department in southwestern France. I was on a working holiday to assist two friends with their garden. They invited me to stay with them on the understanding that I would help clear what was a formidable townhouse jungle. After three days of climbing ladders, hacking away at overgrown trees with a blunt and rusty saw, I descended a rickety wooden ladder in the midday heat to enjoy a glass of cold lemonade. I stooped to take the glass, heard a ominous crack from the base of my spine and felt a bolt of excruciating pain.

I crumpled to my knees and crawled back to the house in agony. Luckily one of my friends who is well known for his hypochondriac tendencies had large quantities of industrial strength painkillers, strong enough to stun a silverback. So ended my gardening duties and thus began my short term addiction to high strength opiates.

With little to occupy myself, apart from reading and puffing on Gauloises, I decided to initiate a plan of action for the remaining days of my stay.

This involved watching as many Netflix series as possible and imbibing a few beers every night at dusk in the local Tabac. The bar could be accessed via numerous routes through the old town, allowing for adventures seeking

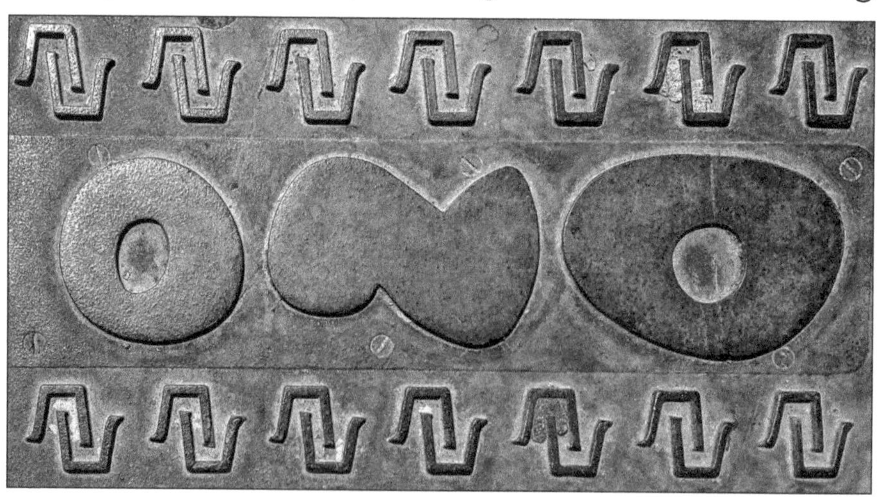

out ancient buildings, including a hidden twelfth century Knights Templar hospital. I walked carefully, anxious to avoid the jarring and jolting of uneven paving stones and raised kerbs.

Eyes cast to the ground, I shuffled gingerly through the winding streets of St-Jean. My downward gaze yielded unexpected delights. Art deco manholes! They adorn the streets and pavements of this now dilapidated town. I was amazed at the craftsmanship of the grids. No matter the size of drains or grids, they held a fascination for me.

Sometimes it was the designs that graced the inspection covers that enthralled me, or in the case of drains simply the basic design concept. Drain covers are not of a universal design. Some have aesthetic qualities that are unexpected in such functional objects.

Their locations and unusual forms fuelled my imagination and led me into magical worlds of giants, aliens and monsters lurking in dark recesses beneath their decorated facades.

HEAVY METAL

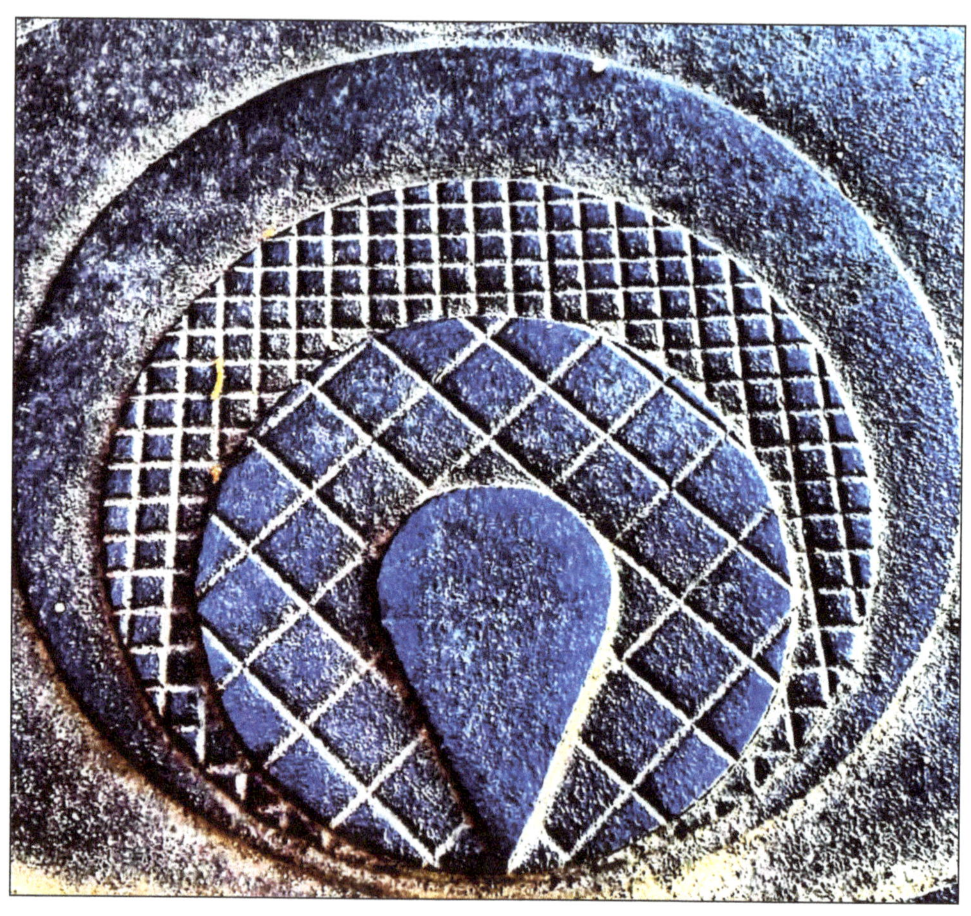

I began photographing the manholes that I encountered on my perambulations to my local sunset watering hole. Over several days of snapping grids I assembled a considerable portfolio of manholes. After showing the images to friends they encouraged me to develop the idea with a view to having an exhibition at some future point.

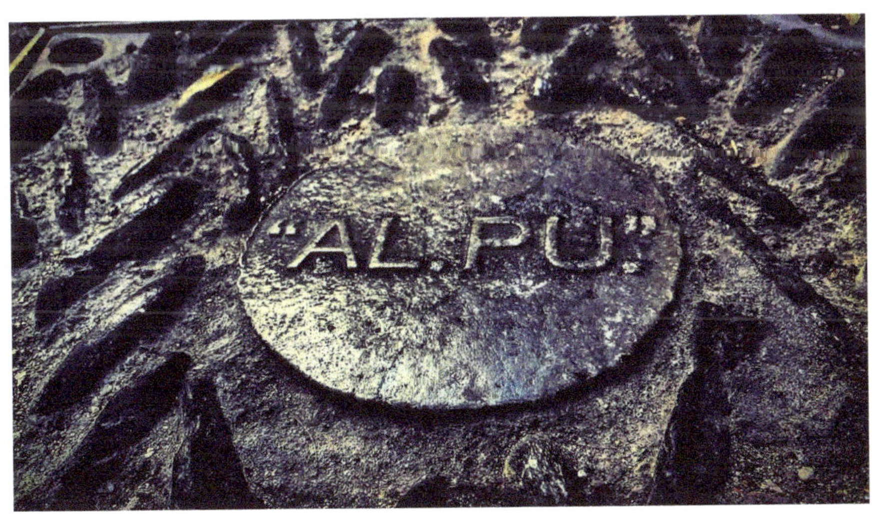

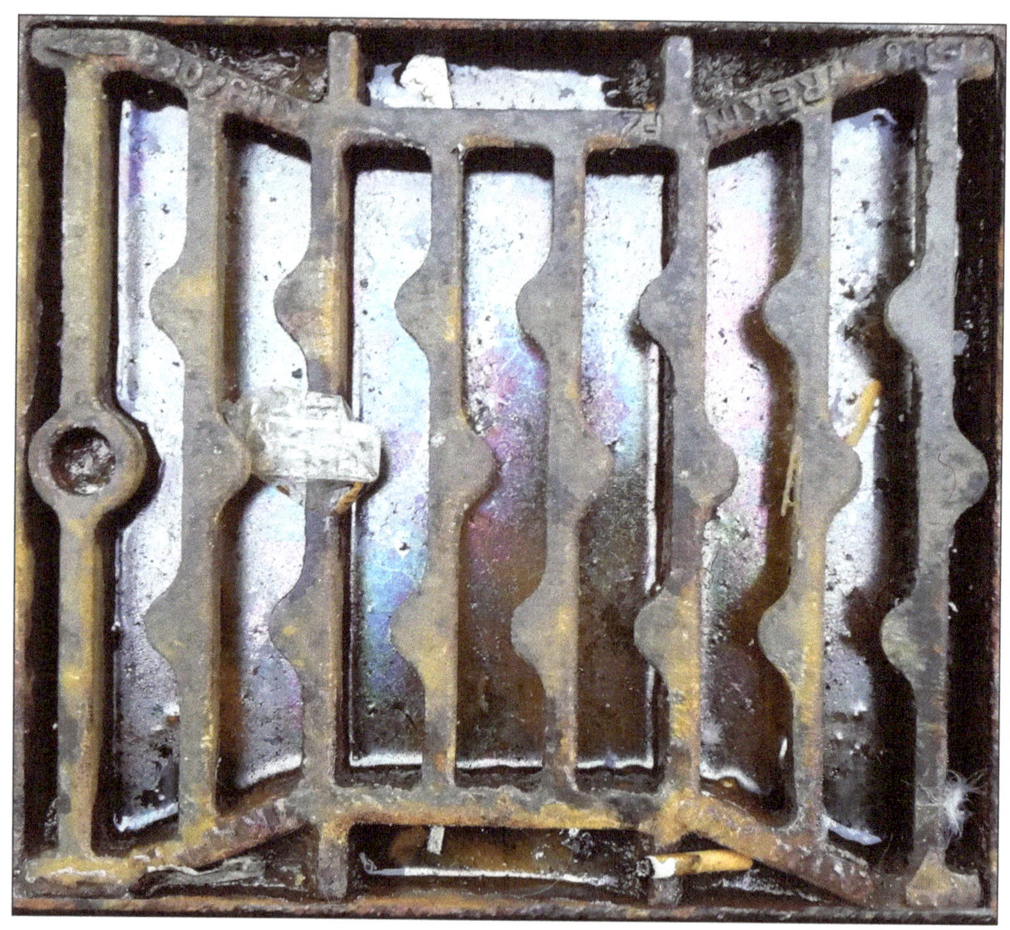

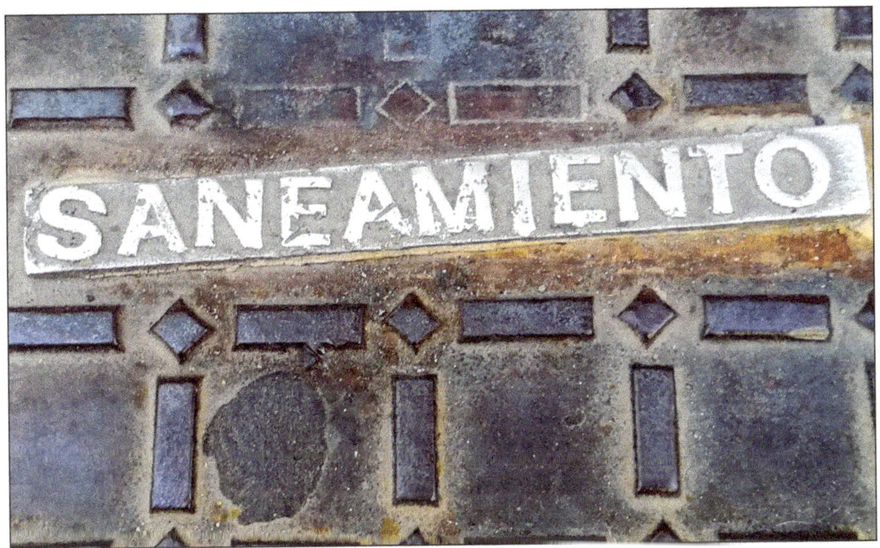

Time passed, a cancer scare and a debilitating illness came and went. After surviving an emotional breakdown and a struggle with depression, I embarked on a series of international travels in search of a new destiny.

It was in Goa Christmas 2017 that I resolved to change my life and follow my creativity. I wasn't sure how I might achieve this but the idea of having an exhibition of manholes was my first step in the journey.

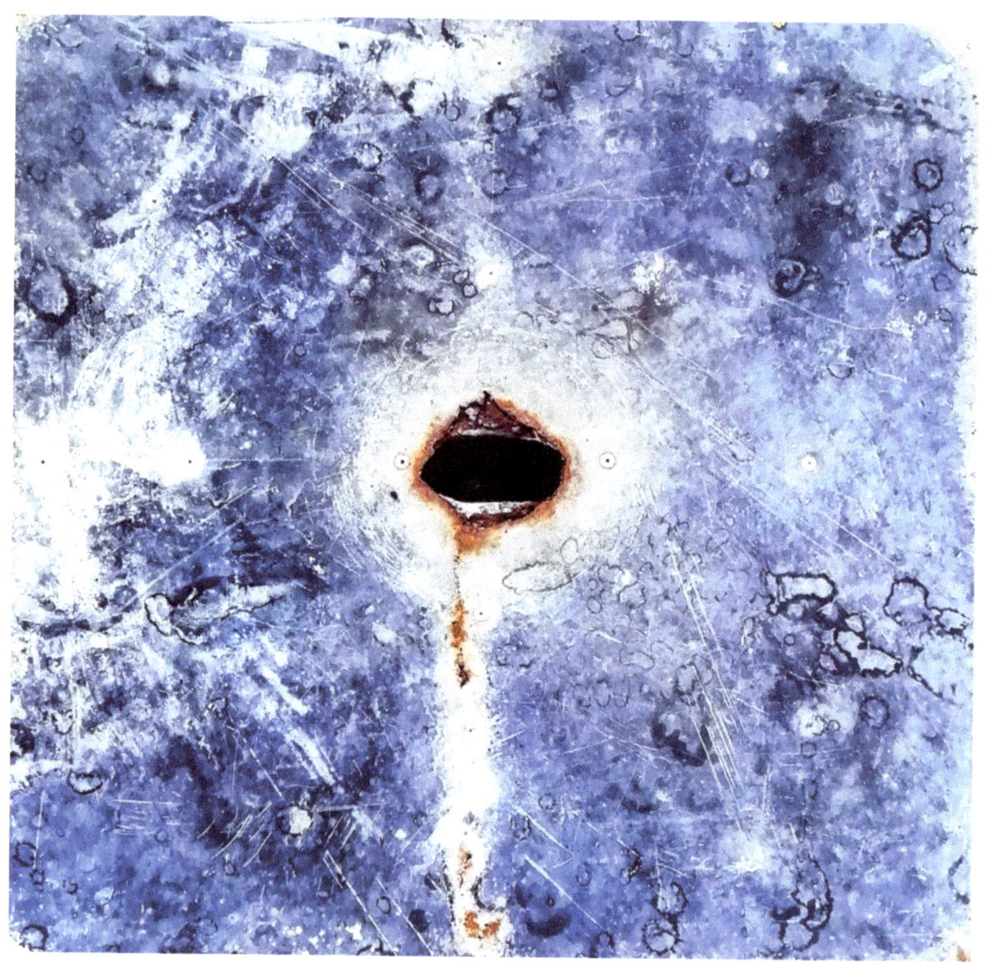

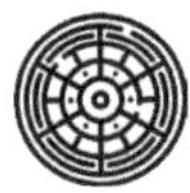

My First Manhole Exhibition

I set about selecting the most impressive images and with the aid of my good friend Bryan Robert Bale, found a printing house and commissioned a set of greeting cards. These would form the basis of a reality check. I wanted to show them to friends in order to assess whether they would be met with interest. The response was encouraging, so I embarked on a search for an exhibition space. Within a month I had secured an offer from Kemi's, an artisan cafe in Pontcanna, a Bohemian neighbourhood of Cardiff.

I had three months to prepare the images. Seventeen photographs were selected to be printed, a few signature pieces on A5 and A4 on foam boards and canvas. Others were in A2 and A3 and sorted into groups. The artwork was printed, a website created and a promotional campaign devised.

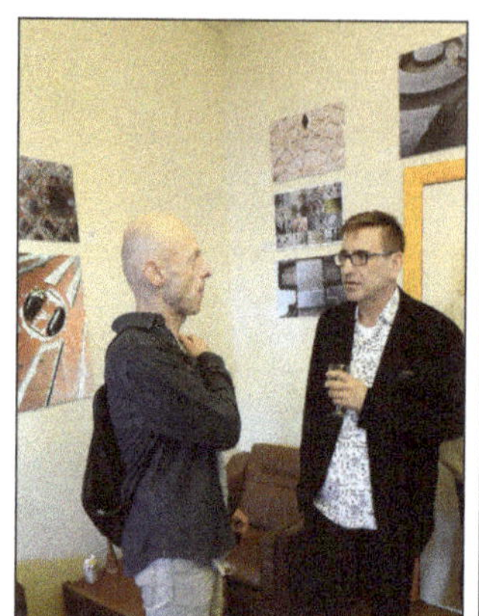

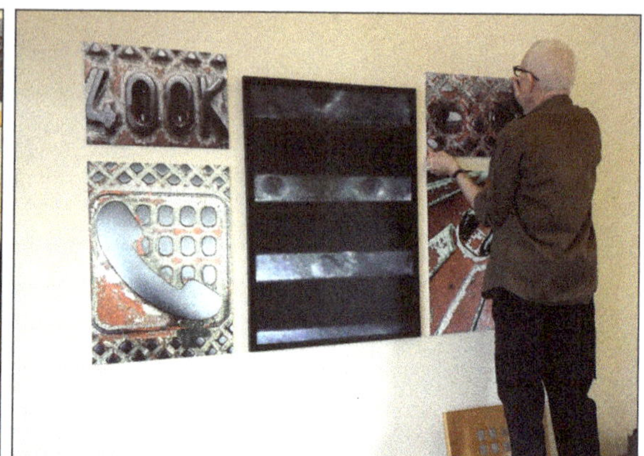
400K

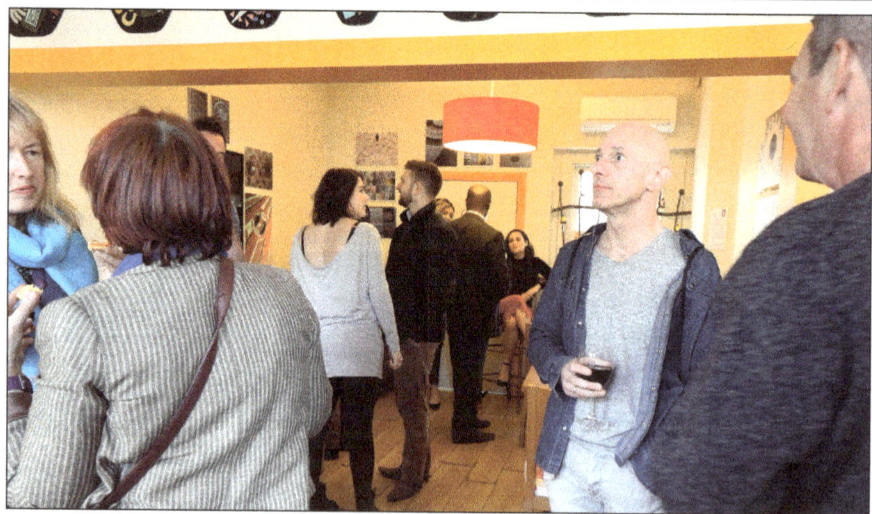

The exhibition was installed on 12th May, my birthday. The preview was attended by 150 people, and I was delighted to have covered my costs and made a profit by the end of the evening.

Jeremy Corbyn, then leader of the Labour Party, was conspicuous by his absence. I forgave him because Britain was in the midst of a general election. If you are wondering why I should brazenly invite him, apparently Mr Corbyn has a passion for decorative manhole covers and drains. I also invited the Mayor of St-Jean-d'Angely. She too was absent. Again, it was an election that thwarted my attempt at entente cordiale.

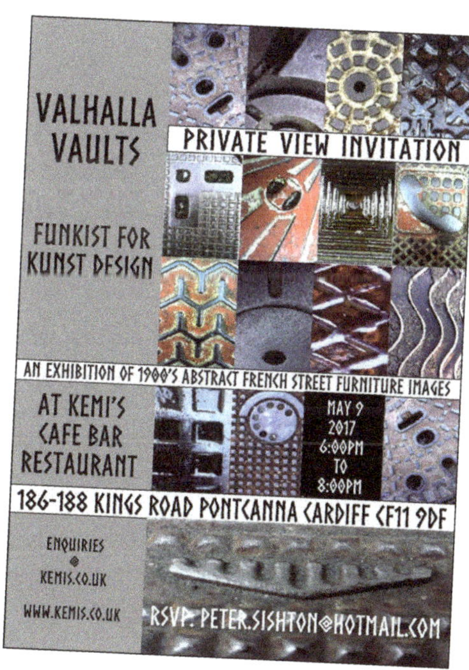

The aim of the exhibition was to celebrate fabulous art forms that adorned the streets of St-Jean.

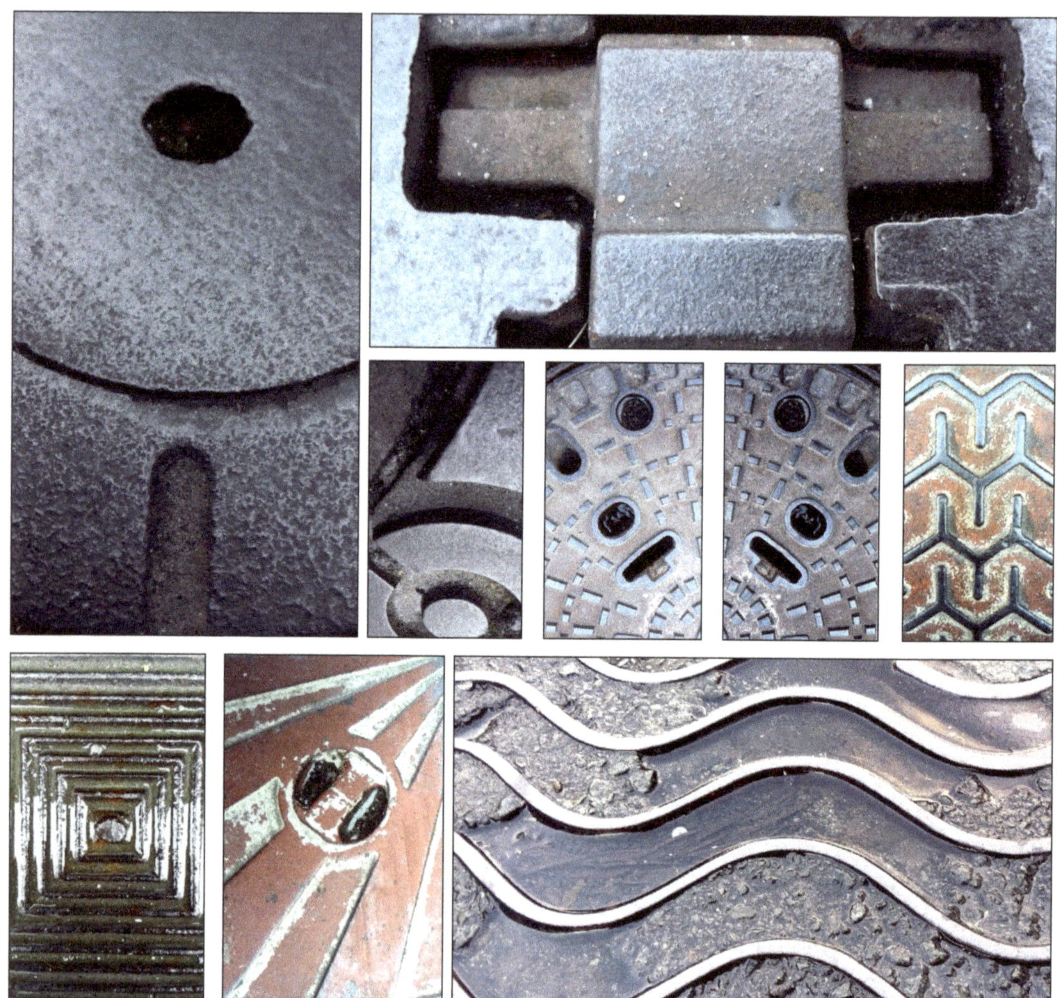

My concept was to present the manholes in their existing state, without manipulation of colour. I wanted to show the images in an abstract form that would intrigue onlookers and challenge them to identify their source.

My interest in manholes continues. It is now three years since my first solo exhibition. I have been contemplating and exploring how I can make a joyful contribution to the appreciation of manholes and their place in the pantheon of art.

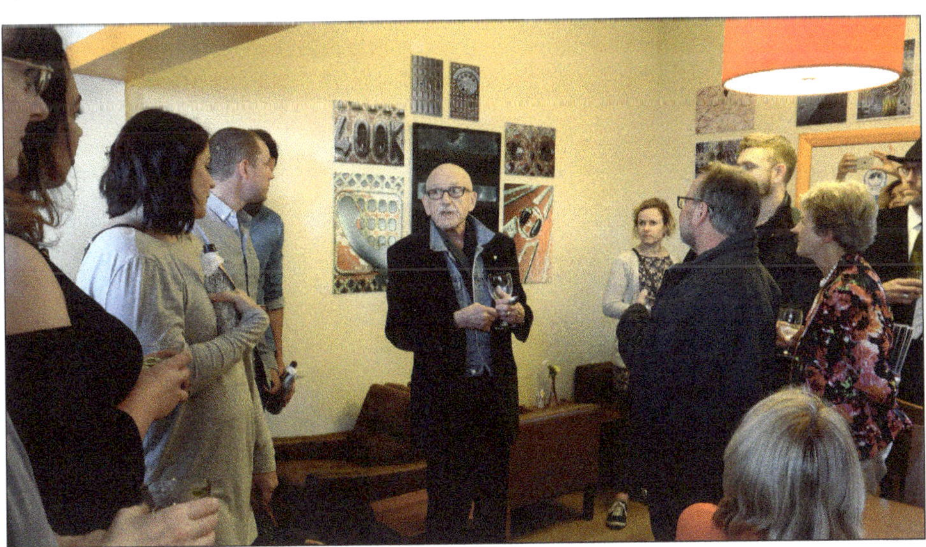

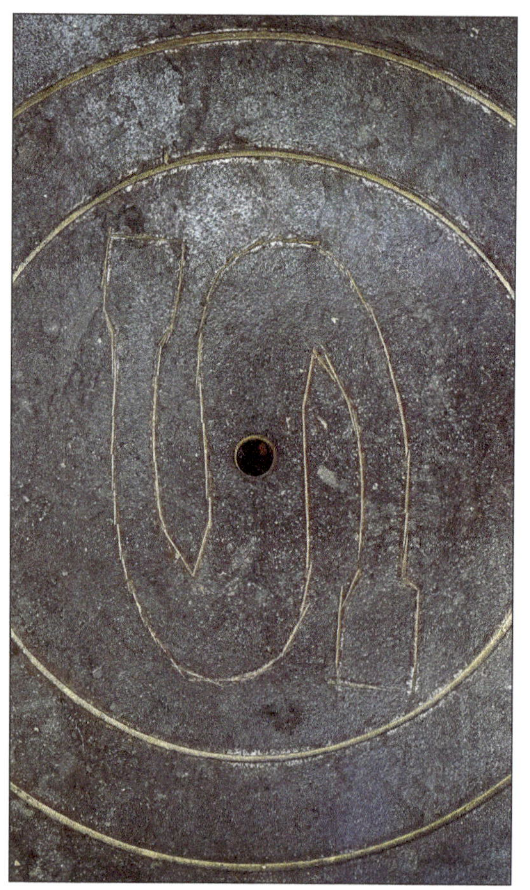

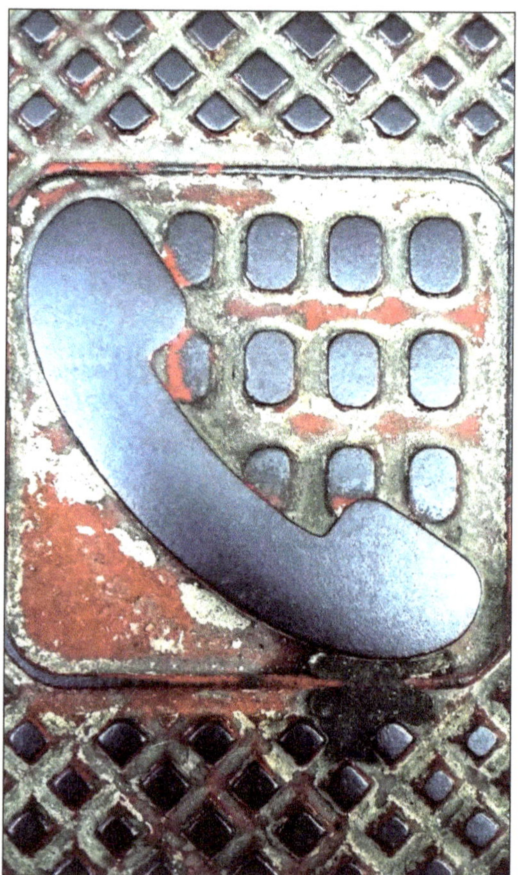

Adventures in Manholes

I have undertaken extensive field work in Spain, the Canary Islands, India and Sri Lanka in search of urban cast iron street art. I should add that field work or rather street work includes many towns, cities and villages in the United Kingdom. Manchester has some splendid examples. I am still stalking the undiscovered holes of this incredible city. Many of these treasures appear in this book. On this occasion I have taken the opportunity to enhance the images so that they embellish the well-trodden designs. After all, many existing manholes are extremely old and deserve a makeover. Moving forward, my interest extends beyond the abstract approach that I took to with my first foray into manholes. I am now exploring how the manholes appear in their various locations. A recent return trip to Seville in Spain in May 2022 provided an exciting opportunity to develop my ideas.

My sojourn to Seville was my first voyage abroad since Covid struck the nation and lockdowns negated any chance of travel. Two years of being limited to the confines of my village was actually not as bad as one might have thought. My eyesight had seriously deteriorated over the period of covid, to the point where I was officially declared blind. Cataracts in both my eyes left me unable to enjoy photography. This inevitably led to depression and frustration. I resolved to bolster my mood by writing my book. It took some effort but I am delighted with the result and I hope that you feel the same. By the time of completion of *Heavy Metal A Tribute to Manholes*, my eyes had worsened to the point that even writing on my PC was impossible. I am pleased that I persevered.

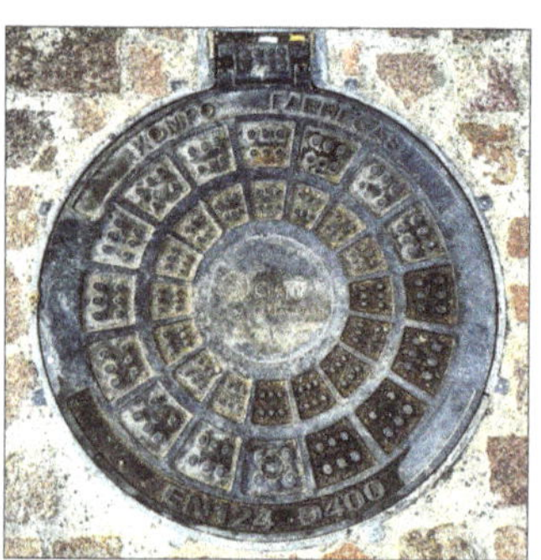
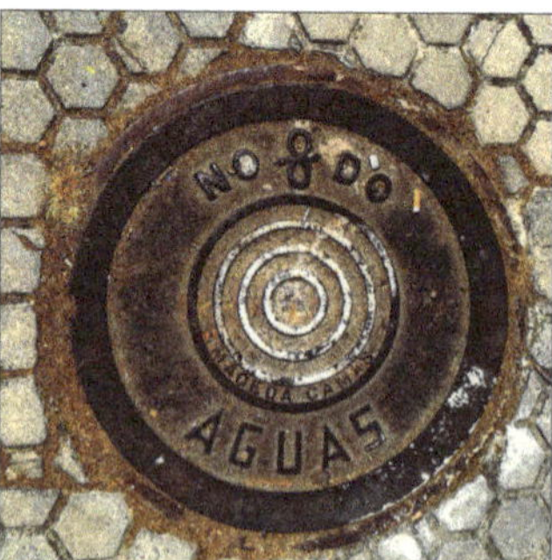

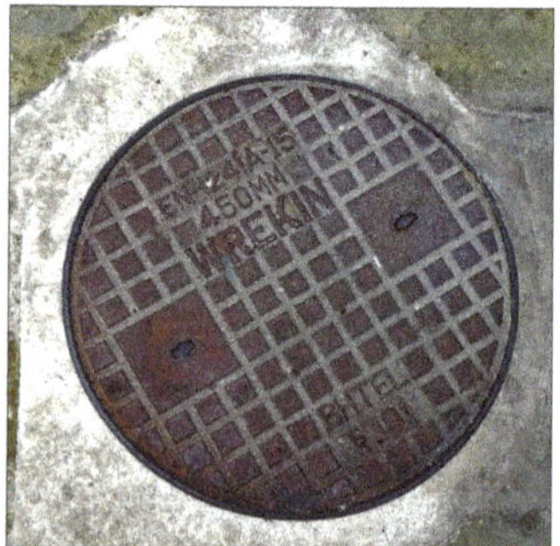

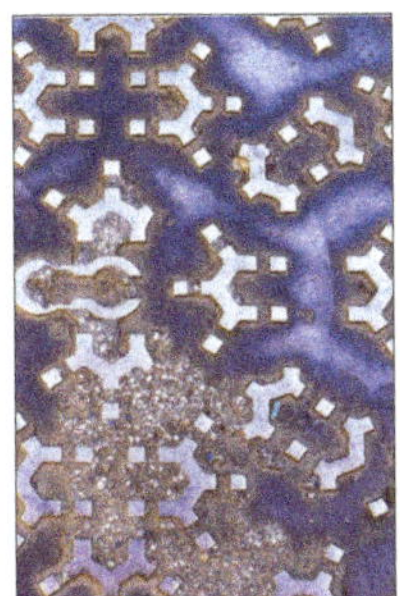
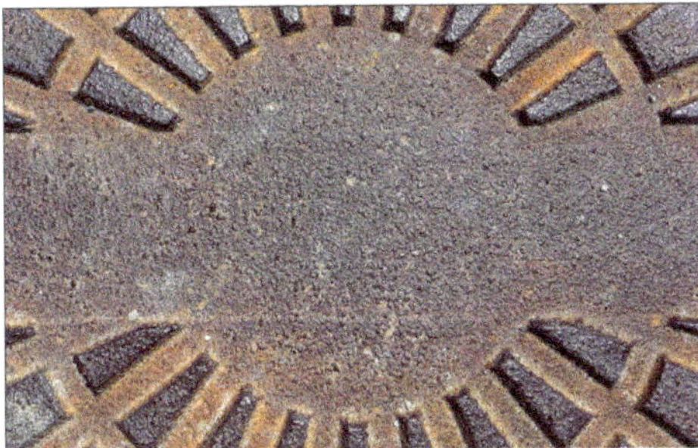
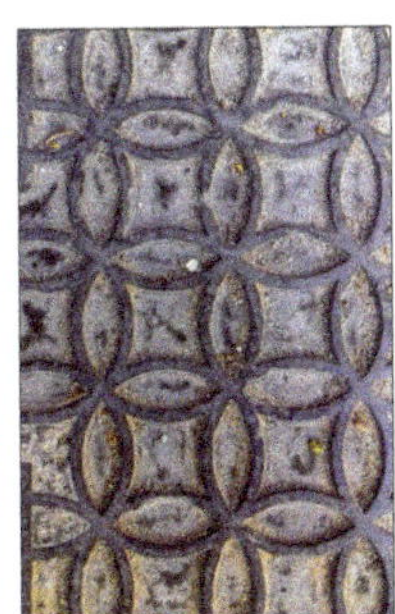

Having researched, written and edited the book, I was ready to approach publishers. This was an anxious time for me. A time of reckoning! Dutifully, and with a modicum of trepidation, four publishers were contacted and submissions made. Within a relatively short period of time, and to my amazement all four publishers responded positively. Unfortunately, two of them required five thousand more words. One publisher required one hundred more images and the other wanted me to contribute funds towards the publishing costs. The idea of writing additional material was not an attractive option because I felt I had already given birth to the narrative and had no wish to create any further material.

I was concerned that I really had very little more to add. Words for words sake in order to meet a quota was not appealing. With regard to images, whilst I have a plethora of photographs in my archive, I was worried about the quality of the images in terms of printability. Remember that I was using my Samsung phone camera. The camera was fine but images taken over the last two years varied in quality, mainly due to my shocking eyesight.

My response to that issue of quality images was to consider taking more photographs. The problem was my poor eyesight. Thankfully the NHS came to my rescue and performed a double cataract operation. With my eyesight returned I purchased a state of the art pocket camera. I could then commence a new project where I explored a new approach to photographing manholes. The initial project of taking abstract images was now complete and I wanted to capture manholes in their environments. A new concept that I found exciting especially with my new camera at hand.

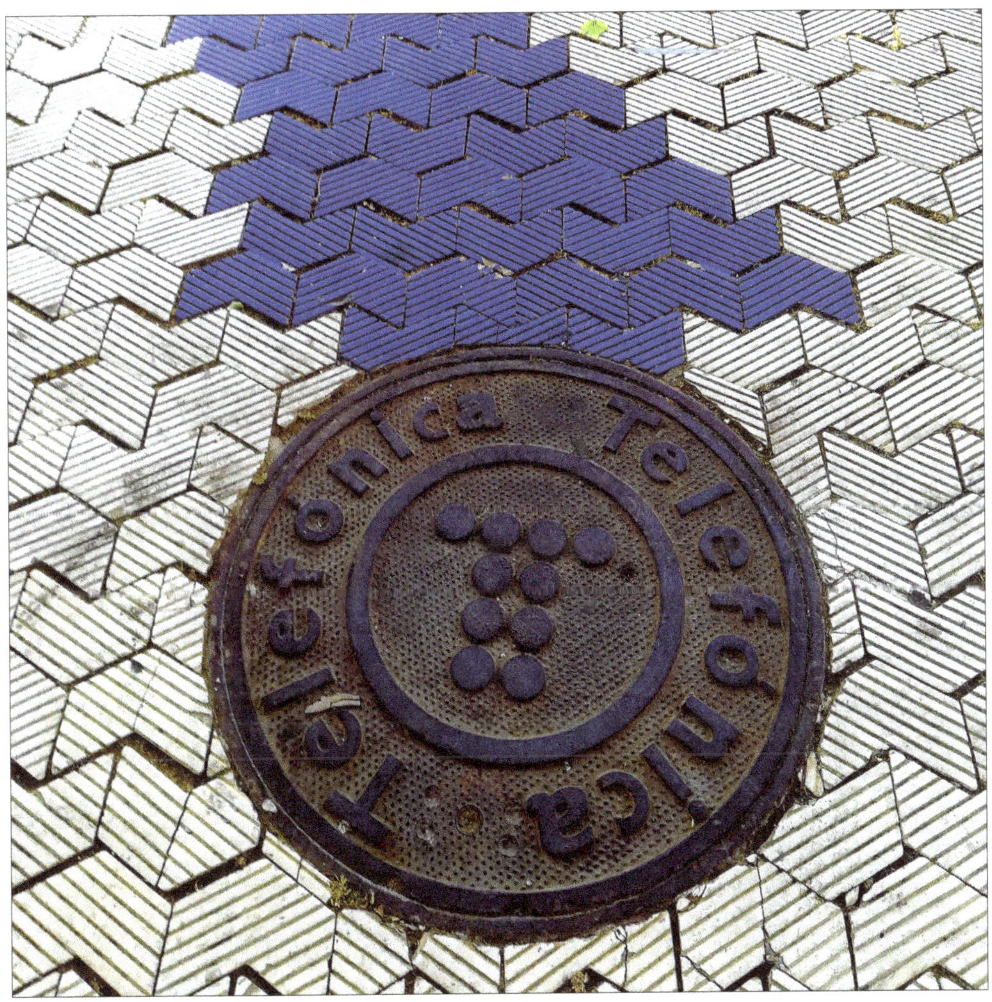
Telefónica Telefónica

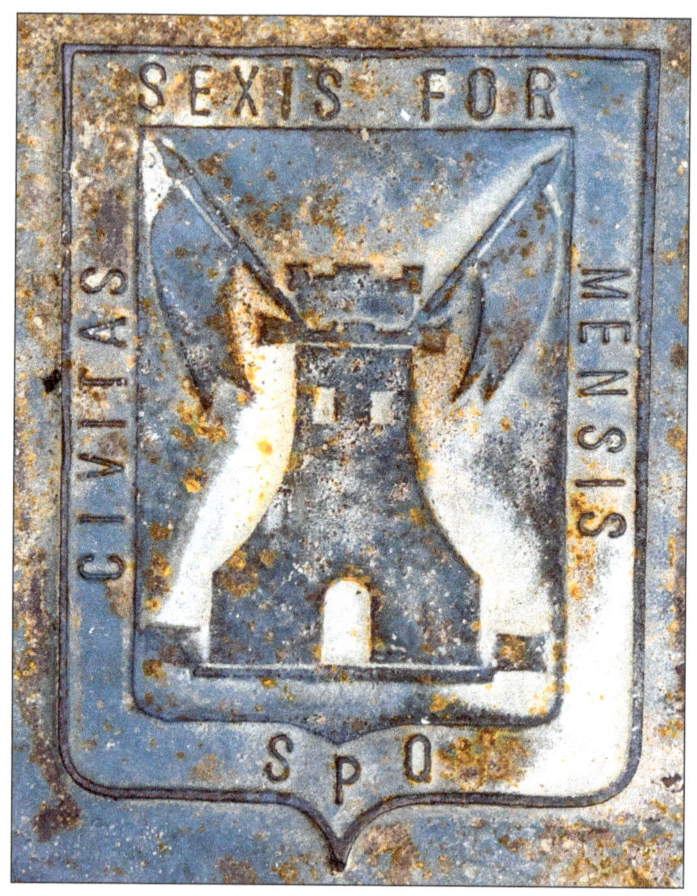
SEXIS FOR
CIVITAS
MENSIS
SPQ

I had started with this new approach using my Samsung phone during my days of limited optical capability. Now I could proceed in the hope that I could enhance my photographic skills and take my art forward and look forward to future results. In May 2022 I went to Seville in Spain to revisit previous manholes in that wonderful city. At the time of writing, I am editing the photographs and I am feeling optimistic at the initial results. I am hoping that a few of the images will appear in the book and most certainly my next exhibition. I have had time to ponder the publishing offers further.

My approach has changed to open up opportunities to ensure that the book is published. I need to make it clear to readers why I wish to be published. Firstly, it's not a vanity project in any way. I refuse to pay publishers, as I do not have the funds nor the ego to do so. Secondly, I entered into the project as a means to healing myself of emotional traumas. Post illness and divorce left me in turmoil and the FunkistKunst project was an important activity in assisting my recovery.

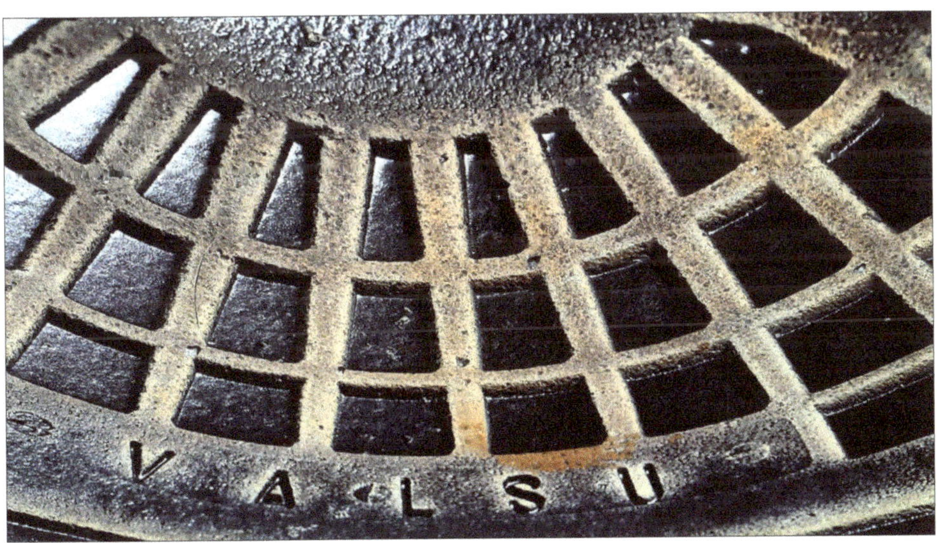

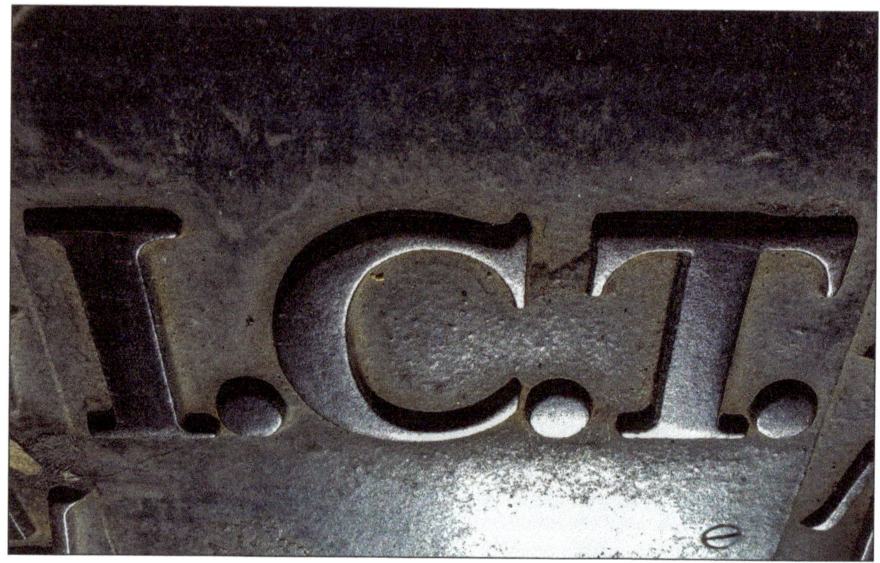

I want to be published because of valid interest not for reasons of vanity. That would undermine the whole idea and undermine my whole intention. Thirdly, when I succeed in being published my intention is to donate any profits to a charity that is close to my heart.

My charity of choice is Survivors Manchester, a fantastically important organisation that provides therapy to male survivors of sexual abuse. Survivors has helped me recover from many years of sexual abuse when I was aged nine to sixteen. One of the many issues that arises out of sexual abuse for me is one of an incredible lack of self esteem. This is a crushingly awful aspect of abuse for me. It has impacted on my education, work and relationships. It is important to me that I feel proud of my achievements, however small they may seem. Survivors have helped me over several years to regain a belief in myself and I do not wish to shatter that progress.

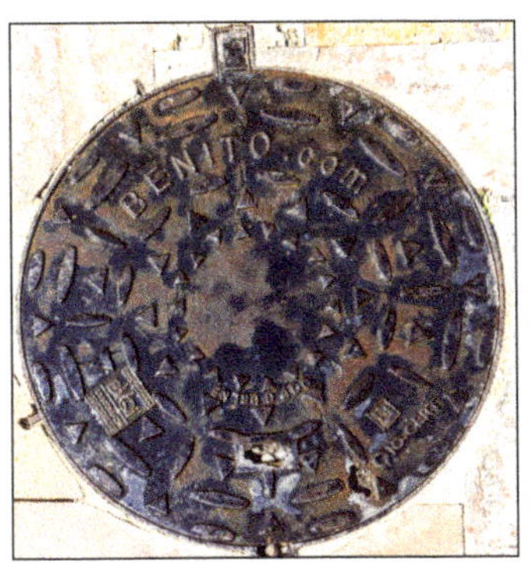

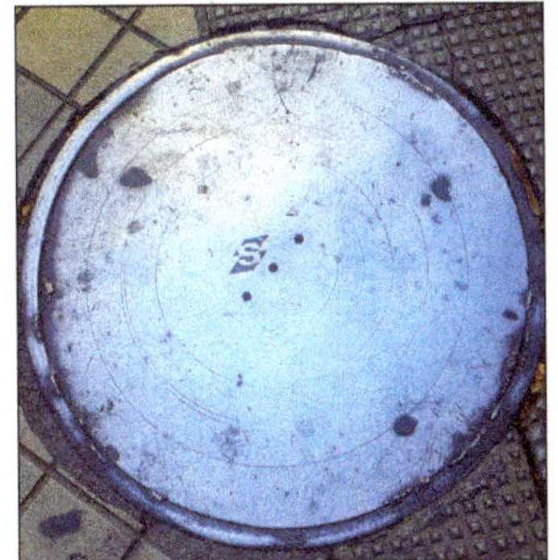

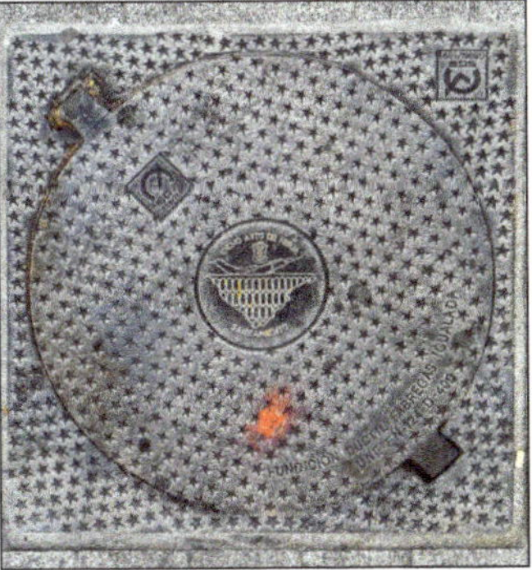

Interestingly, whilst in Seville in May 2022, I had a light bulb moment of another route to being published. Go Fund Me is an online app that allows individuals to seek financial contributions from individuals from around the world. With that in mind, I took to the streets of Seville with the intention of creating a portfolio of new images that could be used in Go Fund Me calls for support. I launched my campaign during May 2022 and by July had accrued a healthy amount of donations and at the time of writing have secured half of the publishing costs. I am hopeful that donations will continue over the coming months. Interestingly, when I had completed the first draft of *Heavy Metal A Tribute to Manholes* I had the thought of approaching manhole manufacturers to see if their marketing teams might be interested in sponsoring me. I approached five UK based manufacturers and I was delighted to receive initial interest from two of them. Sadly neither were willing to proceed, citing covid as a reason but both wished me luck! At this moment, I am writing a second draft, giving birth to additional narratives in the hope that I might even get to the magic ten thousand words required by the two non-vanity publishers. I am also hopeful that the new photographs from Seville will be of sufficient number to provide the street art publisher with the additional images to meet their requirements. I do not give up easily.

I hope you find these inspiring and creative designs a delight. May your walks down town and city streets never be the same again.

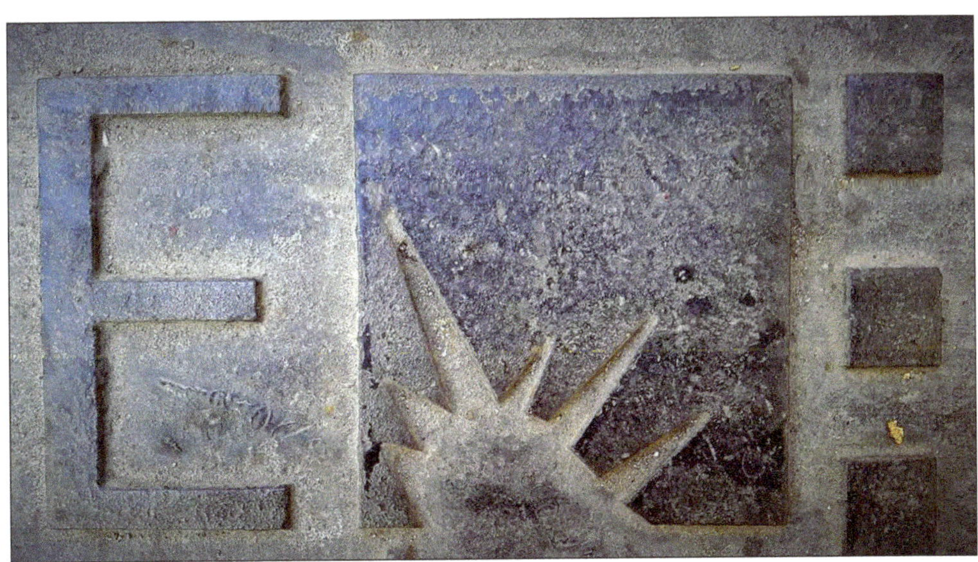

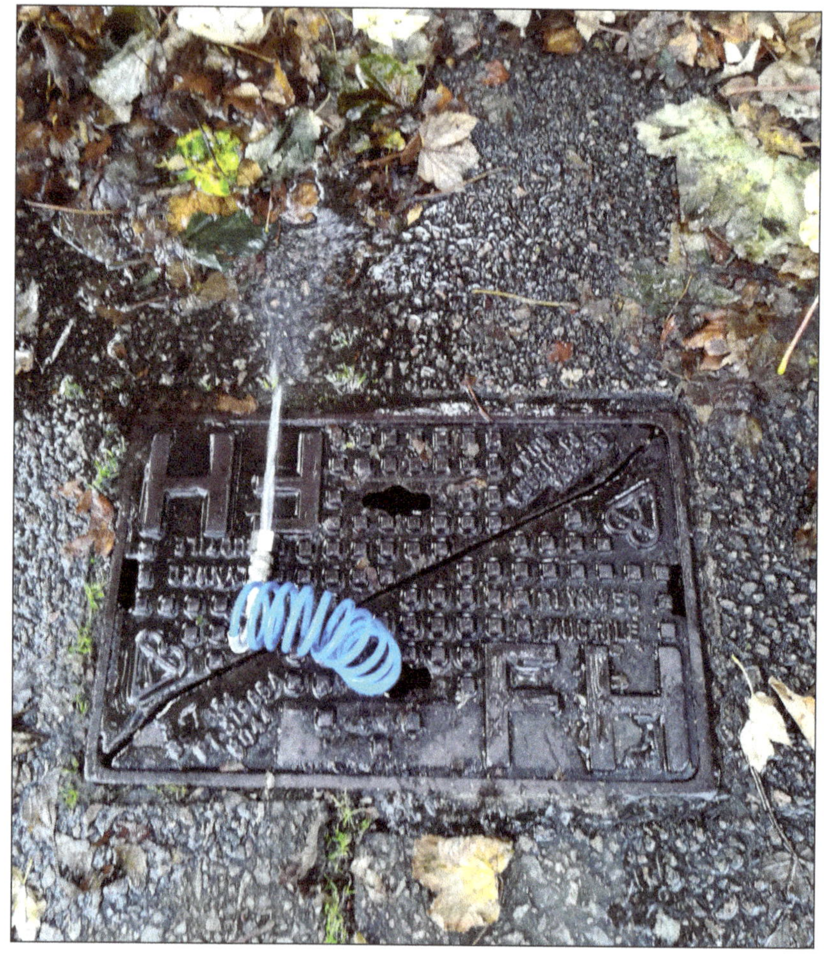

Overview

For many, discussion of what are commonly called manholes is limited to conversations relating to the effects of global warming, in particular flooding. Feckless individuals littering the streets combined with local authority cuts reducing maintenance costs have led to frequent floods, due to drains blocked with leaves and garbage.

For those with an eye to the ground however, drains and manhole covers, or for those with a sensitive disposition, inspection covers, provide a fabulous form of street art. Manholes or grids exist all over the world and at their best exhibit wonderful design patterns, shapes and colours. At their worst, they can rust and slash flesh, or disintegrate leaving treacherous holes in streets or pavements. Not many people are privileged to have discovered the delights that manholes hold, but for those who care to look down they will be amazed at the glorious variety of urban industrial art that lies beneath their feet.

Manholes are gateways to a subterranean world of telephonic cables, sewers and power cables. They often provide glimpses of history, denoting their manufacturing source, their foundries of birth, or celebrate the city or town where they exist. Granada in Spain for example has many “agujeros de hombres” that denote the city's heraldic symbol, the Pomegranate. These are often in brass that glitter gold in the sunshine.

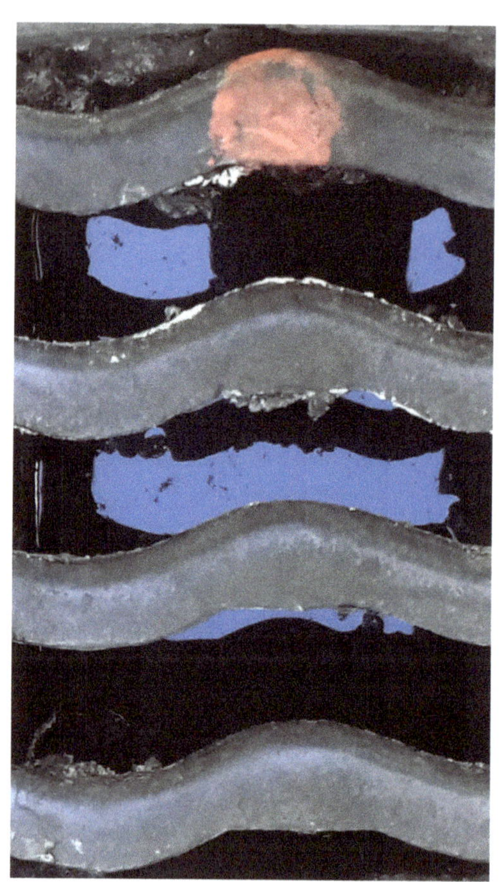

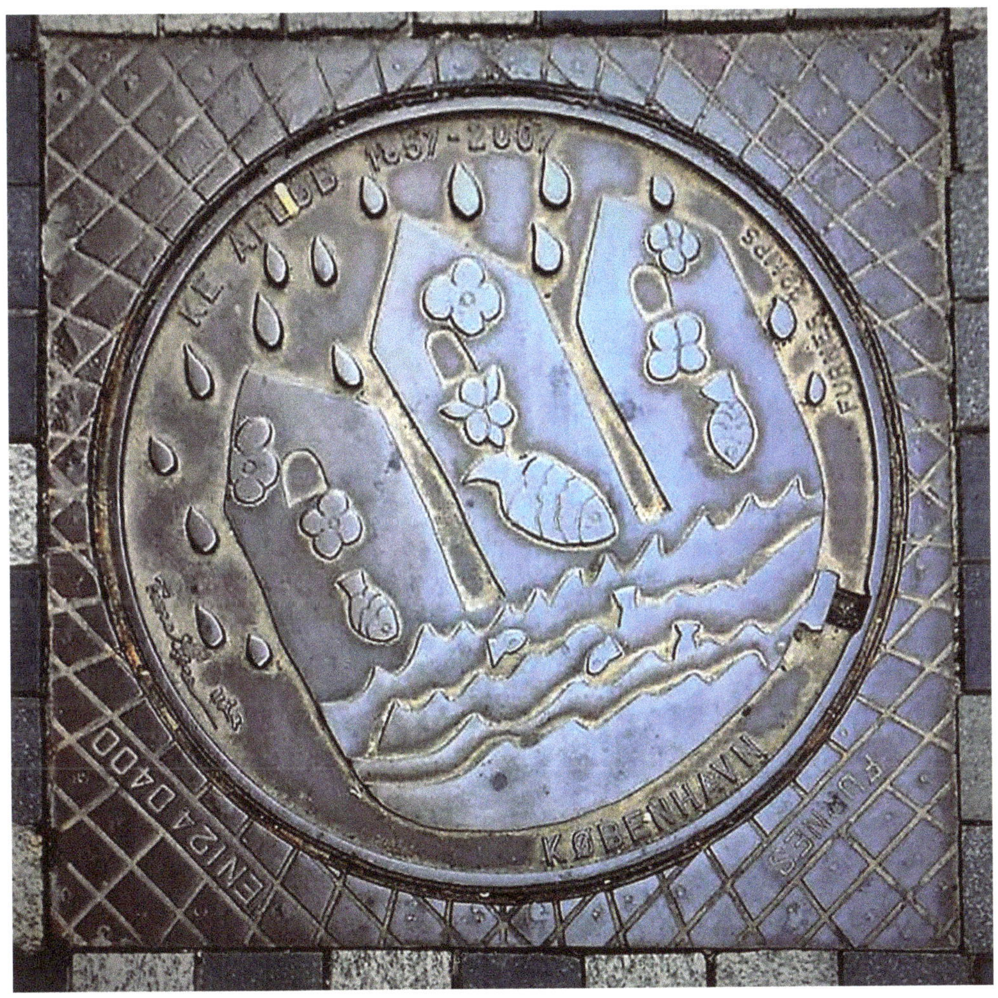
KØBENHAVN
FURNES
EN124 D400

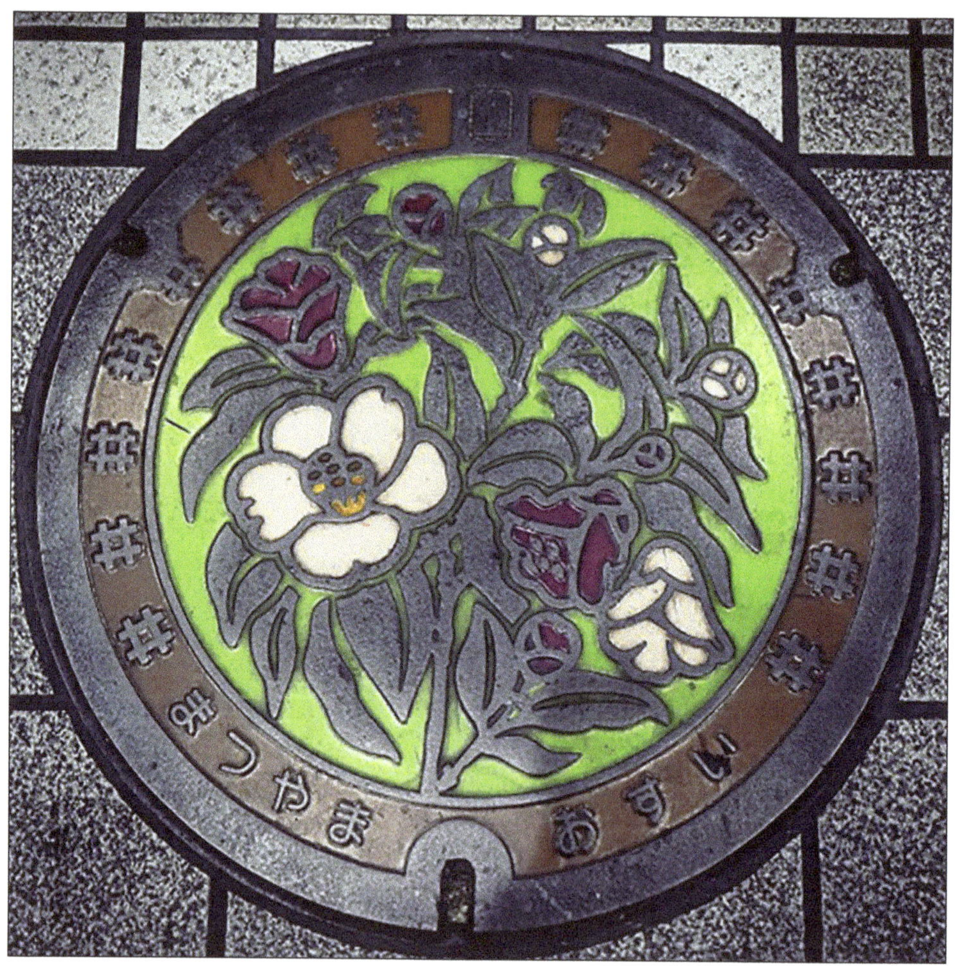
まつやま
おすい

Japan is renowned for its customised manhole covers, commissioned in the 1980s, to encourage the population to embrace major subterranean public works. The design quality is off the scale, their form is intricate or bold and often in colour.

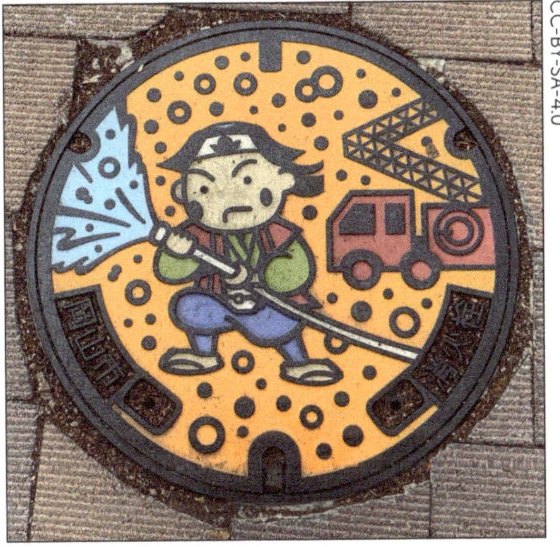

Manhole covers in Okayama prefecture

One might argue that Japan's efforts put most other countries' attempts at covers into the shade. This is not necessarily always the case. Denmark boasts elaborate lids and parts of France and Spain also have splendid examples. I am not a world expert on covers, so I apologise if I have offended any country by omission.

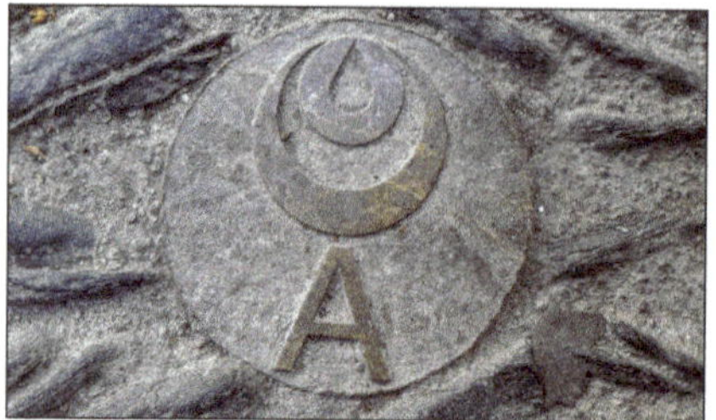

The variety and shapes are infinite, some convex, others perforated. Their design and form are astonishing. They include raised metalwork nodules, crosses, arrows, stars, flora and fauna.

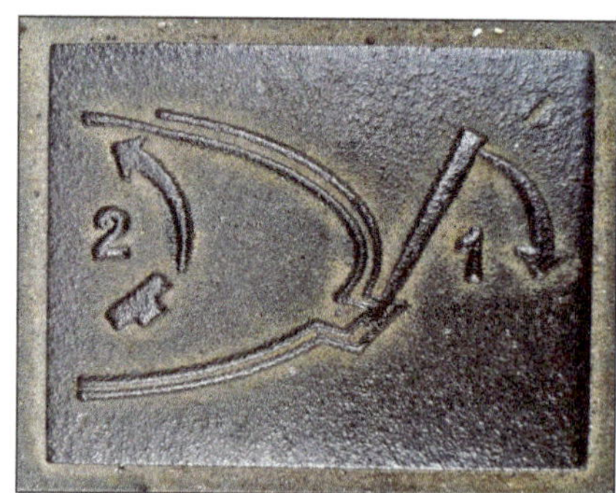

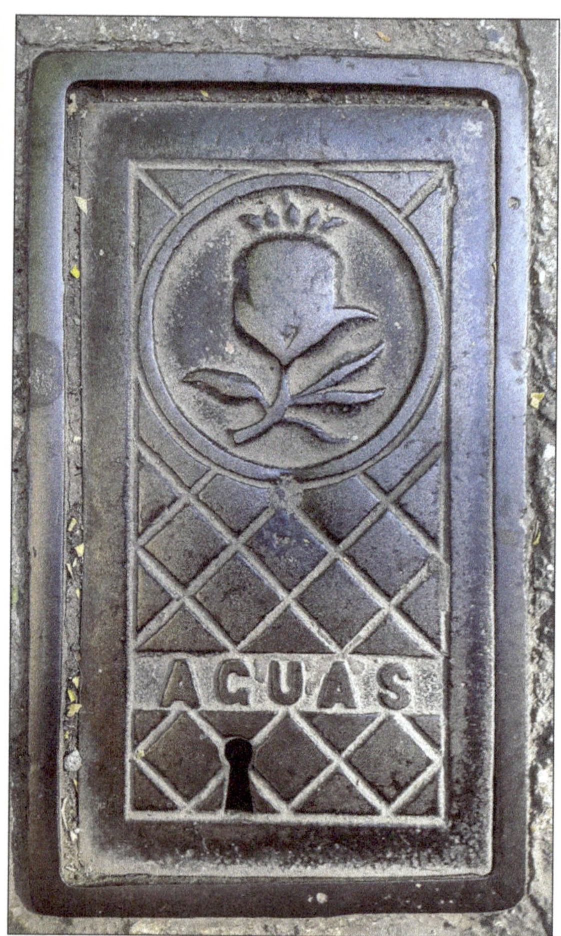

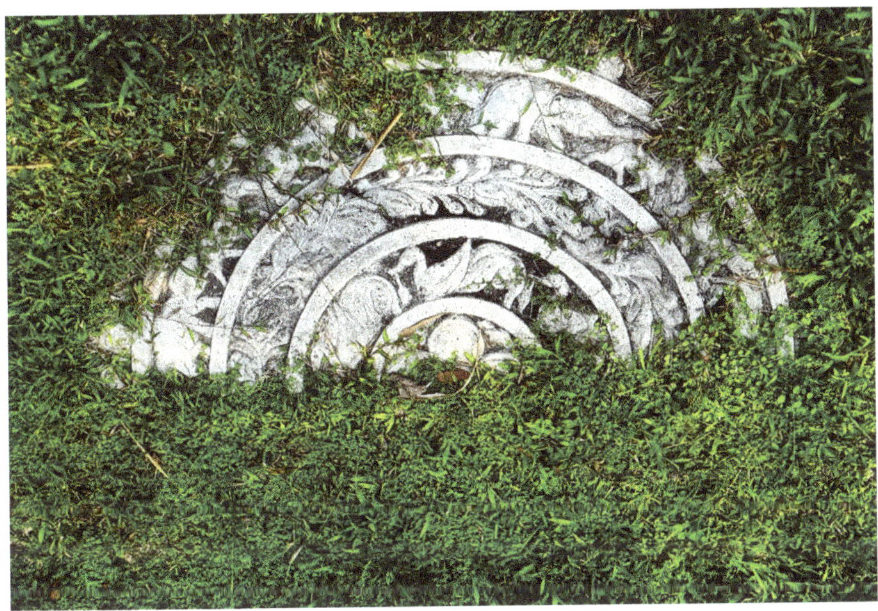

At their best they provide multitudes of images for the discerning public to admire. There is a wonderful example of Berlin t-shirt artists who have elevated street art from the ground to chest level, and print manholes onto clothing. Not least, manholes often provide an historical record of amazing craftsmanship from around the globe.

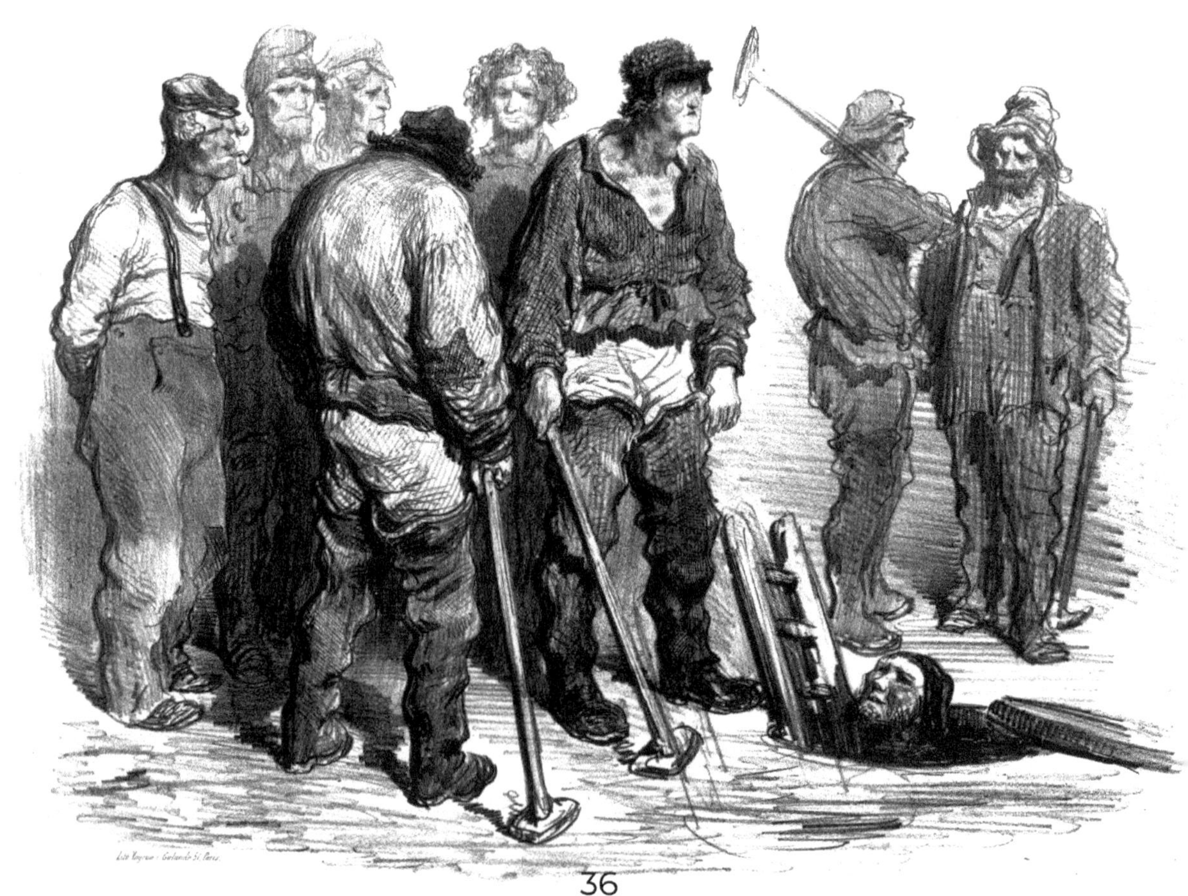

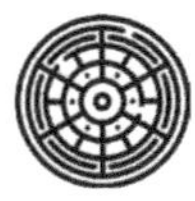

A BRIEF HISTORY OF MANHOLES

As previously mentioned, the term manhole may not appear to be politically correct to some people. However, the word has been in common usage since these objects began to proliferate in the world's cities. This dates back to the beginnings of the industrial revolution, when cast iron covers were introduced to provide access to underground chambers and spaces. Manholes have acquired alternative descriptors that include utility holes, cable chambers, maintenance holes and grids. The name "manhole" is sometimes changed to make it gender neutral. The city of Berkeley, California, for example, changed the official term to "maintenance hole" in 2019. For reasons of historical accuracy I will refer to manholes as manholes in this book.

Manholes are often used as an access point for an underground public utility, allowing inspection, maintenance, and system upgrades. The majority of underground services have manholes, including water, sewers, telephone, electricity, storm drains, district heating and gas.

Manholes are generally found in urban areas and less frequently in rural settings. In rural areas, services such as telephone and electricity are usually carried on utility poles or pylons rather than being underground.

We can thank the Romans for manholes! In 1912 a limestone sewer covering dating from the first century AD was excavated in Vindobona (present-day Vienna.) If you are planning on visiting Vienna you can see this ancient artefact in the Roman Museum of Vindobona.

Roman manholes were made of wood or stone and were not as robust as the ones we are familiar with today. In those times covers didn't have to contend with the thunderous pounding of juggernauts and heavy vehicles.

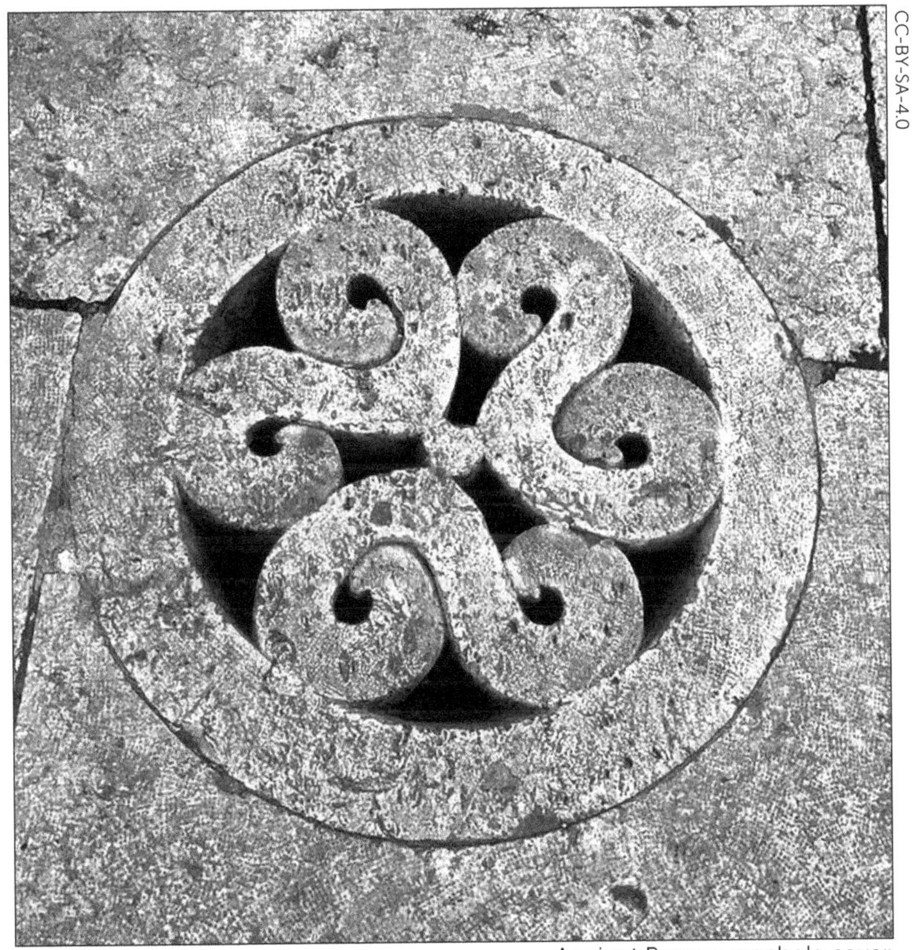

Ancient Roman manhole cover

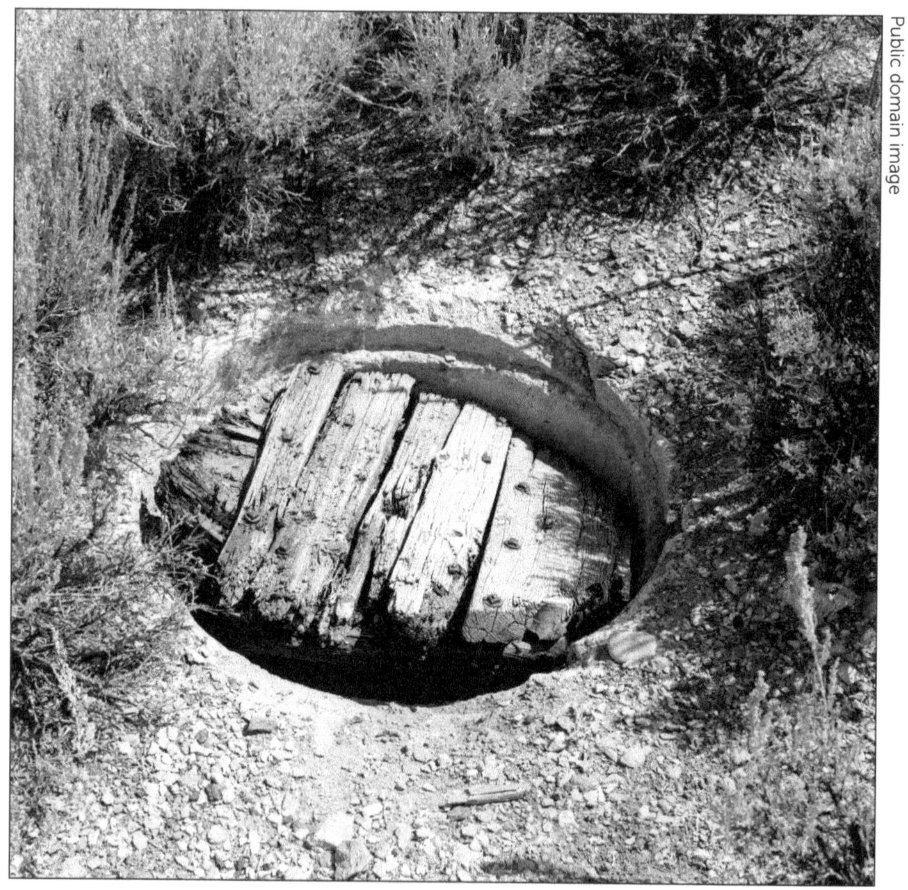

Public domain image

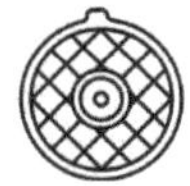

Back to today

These days they are made of sturdier materials and are often composed of cast iron, and sometimes concrete or steel. Due to European health legislation (manual handling weights) some are now made of lighter composite materials, with an added benefit of having electrical insulating properties and greater slip resistance.

Research suggests that the average weight of a manhole is usually 113 kilograms (249 lb). Their heaviness and composition protects against the constant battering they receive from heavy traffic, saving maintenance and replacement costs, whilst also helping to ensure they remain in place.

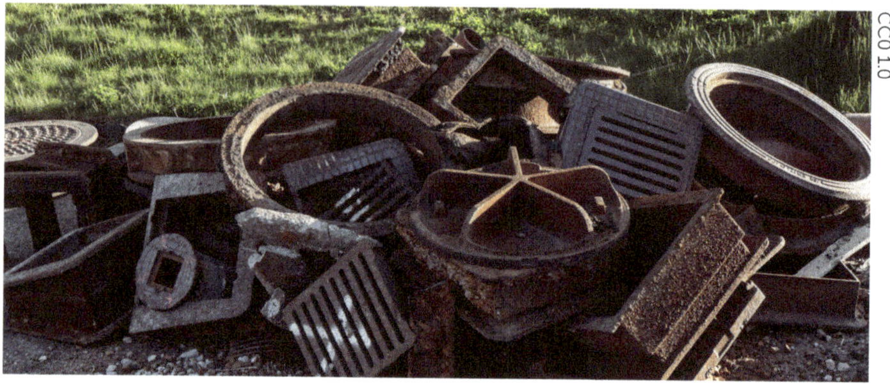

Considering their formidable weight and visibility I find it incredible that theft is becoming a problem worldwide. An amazing 240,000 manhole covers were stolen in Beijing in 2014. How does one pilfer a manhole without detection? You can hardly stick a manhole up your jumper or bury it beneath a blanket in a pram. It would buckle your knees or wheels and be highly conspicuous. Why on earth would people want to steal them?

I guess one reason might be their value in terms of scrap metal. Another may be an unrelenting passion for them as objects of beauty. I admit to my predilection for manholes but draw the line at theft.

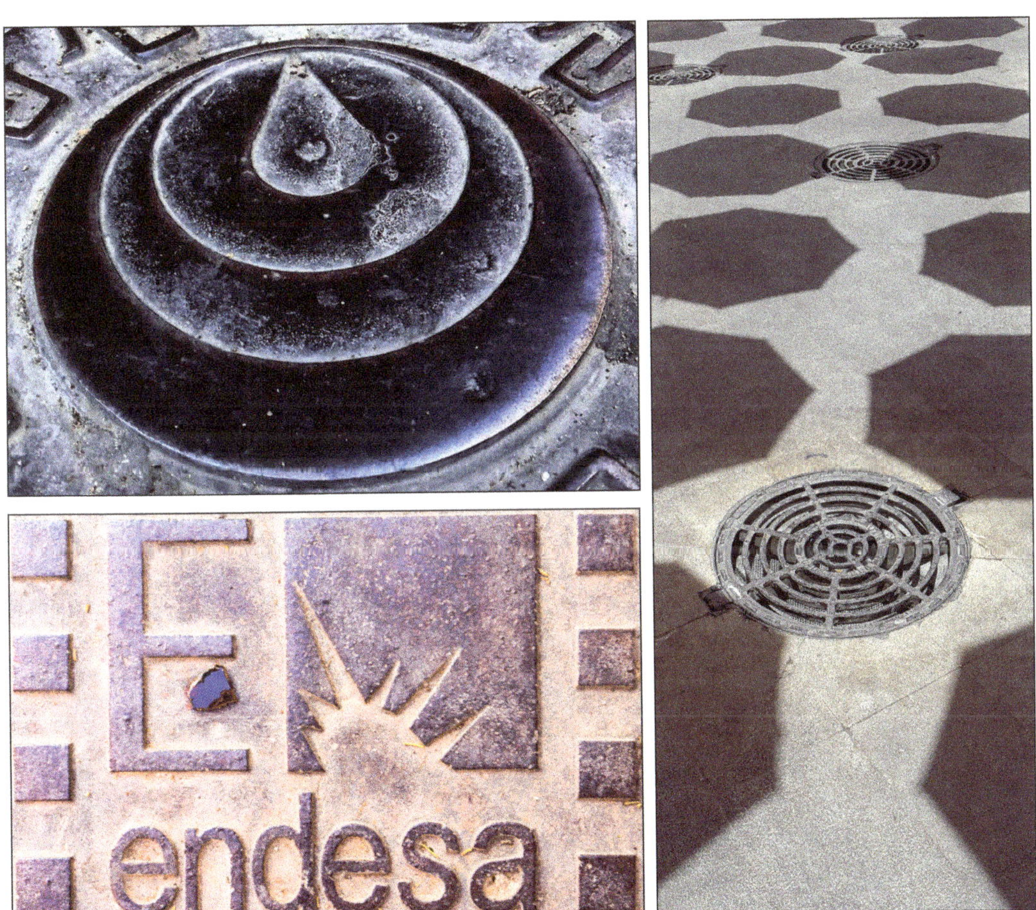
E
endesa

In East London, a decade after its installation, a manhole cover designed by artist Antony Gormley was stolen, the manhole equivalent of a Banksy theft?

Given the fact manhole theft is on the rise, it is surprising that there are few reported incidents of death by falling down uncovered manholes. In India there are a couple of harrowing news reports of young children losing their lives in this way whilst playing. Hopefully the chances of falling down a manhole and meeting one's doom is about as likely as winning the lottery. Let's hope so.

If you care to ask anyone if they have ever fallen down a manhole, you may well be surprised at their reply. I mention this because that question was asked of me recently. My answer? Yes I have! I was fortunate, thankfully a chubby Hells Angel had disappeared down it a few seconds before my rapid descent.

The incident happened at night, with no street lighting. Alcohol was partially to blame. The question was posed by someone who had also fallen into a manhole.

More recently a friend recounted his story of when he attended an adult education class at a college in Cardiff. He had reported to reception to enrol and was told to proceed through some double doors. As he did so, suddenly he found himself hurtling downwards and found himself amongst a plethora of pipes and wires. Just as he was pondering what on earth had happened a concerned face appeared above him. It was the college janitor.

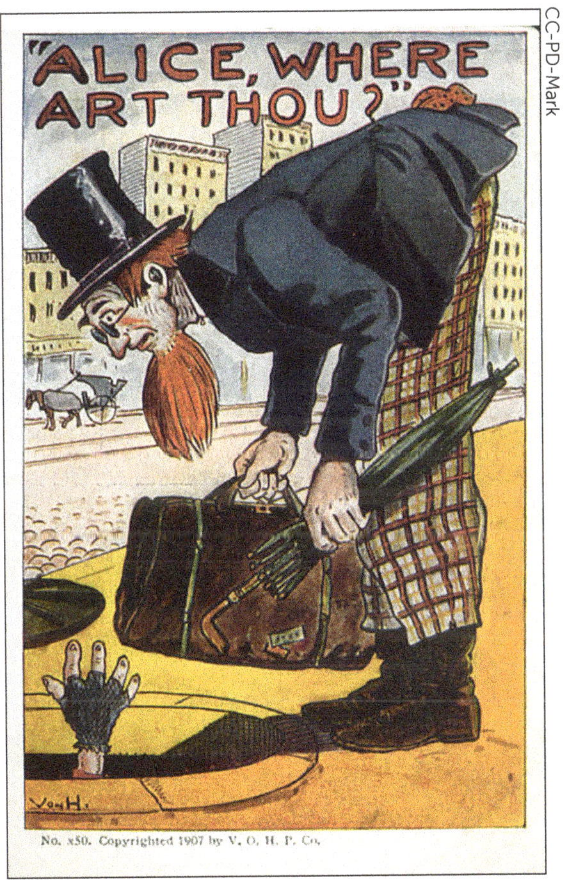

He had removed the manhole cover in the downstairs corridor and before he could place warning signs around the gaping hole, my unwitting friend had descended, thankfully without serious injury.

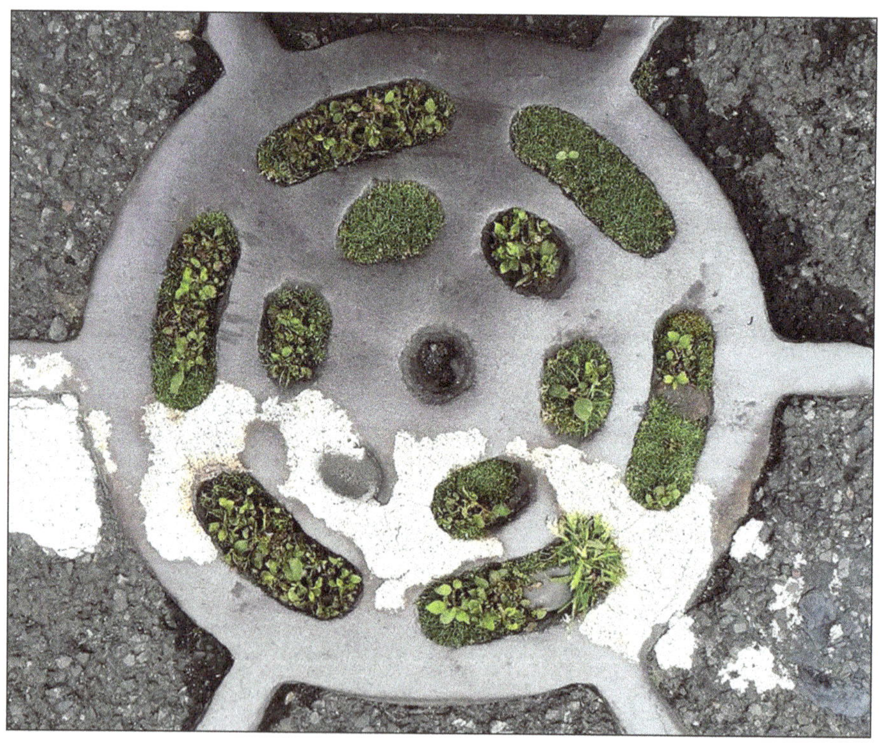

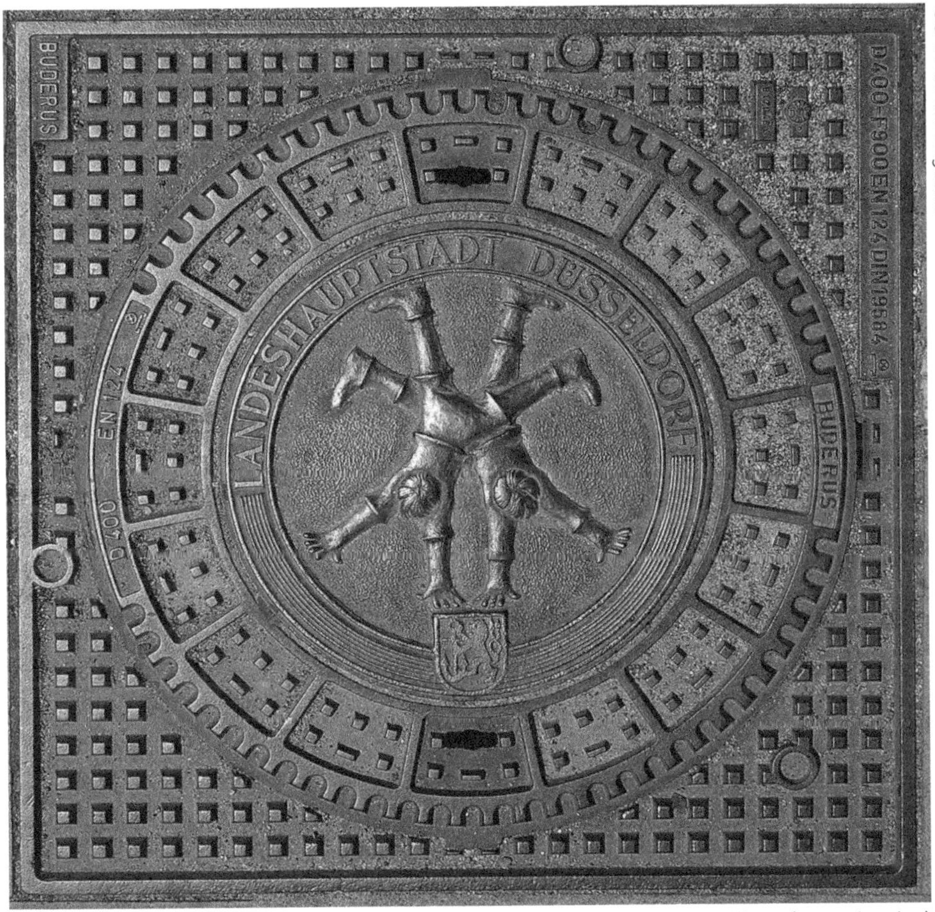

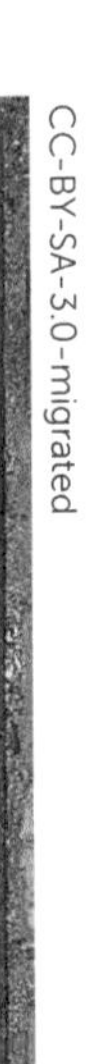

Düsseldorfer Radschläger (cartwheeler)

In the early hours of the morning I find myself pondering how many manholes exist in the world. Perhaps this is like asking how many stars there are in the universe, or how many grains of sand exist on beaches, beneath seas and oceans of our planet. It's mind boggling! I suspect that mind boggling is exactly what job applicants for Microsoft were when asked the following question, "Why are manholes round?".

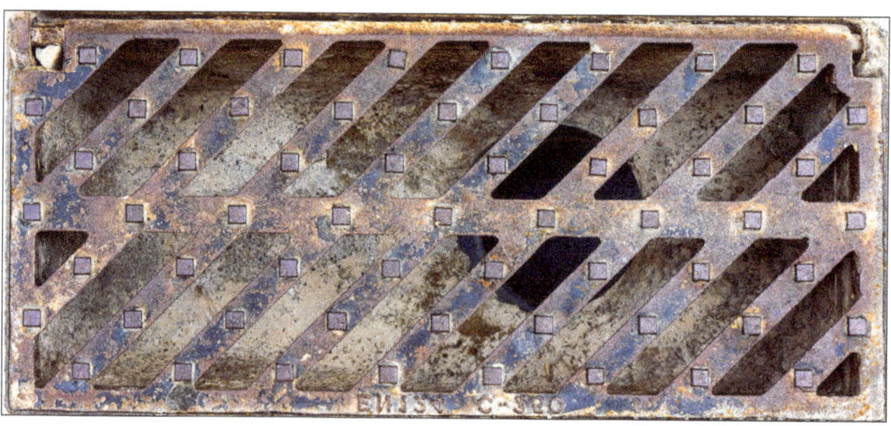

There are numerous answers that could be considered correct. Answers on a postcard please!

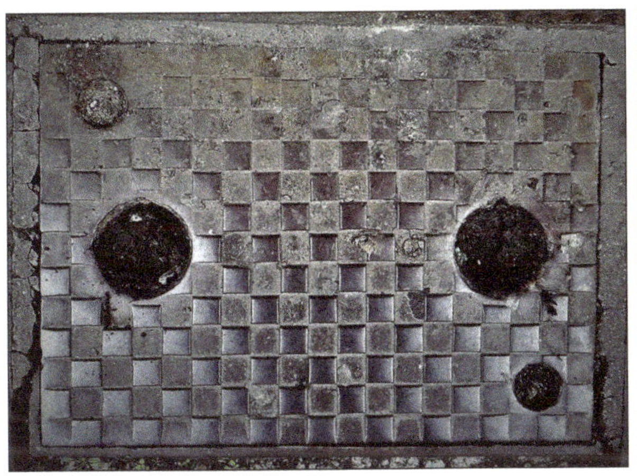

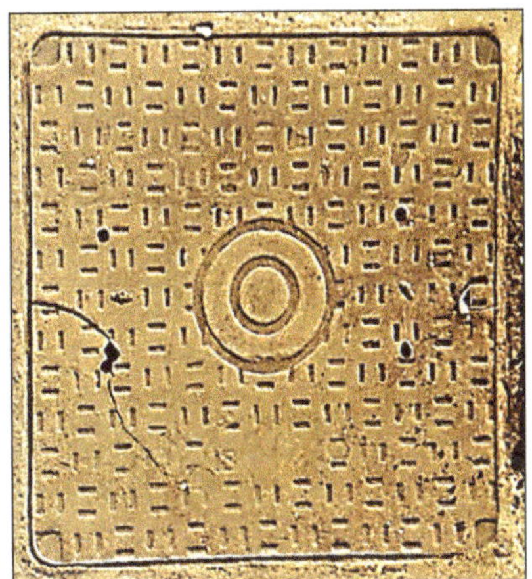

Actually, not all manholes are circular, so why are manholes oblong, square or rectangular? For those of you pondering the reason for round holes, one could consider them to be easier to manoeuver. Think of a patent for square wheels? Now there's a thought.

There have been a number of unusual incidents that have come to my notice with regard to manholes. Most notably the time a manhole cover was unexpectedly launched into space in the 1950s.

The story goes that during operation Plumbob, a 900 kg manhole cover was blasted into the atmosphere during an American nuclear test. A scientific observer, when asked how fast the inspection lid was travelling, stated that " photographic evidence suggests it was going like a bat out of hell!

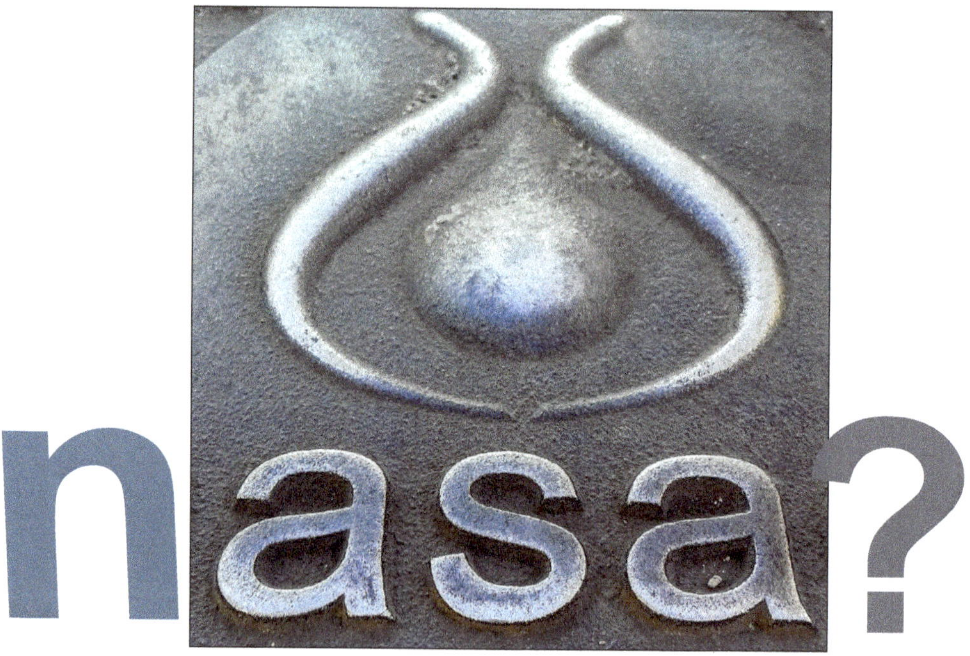

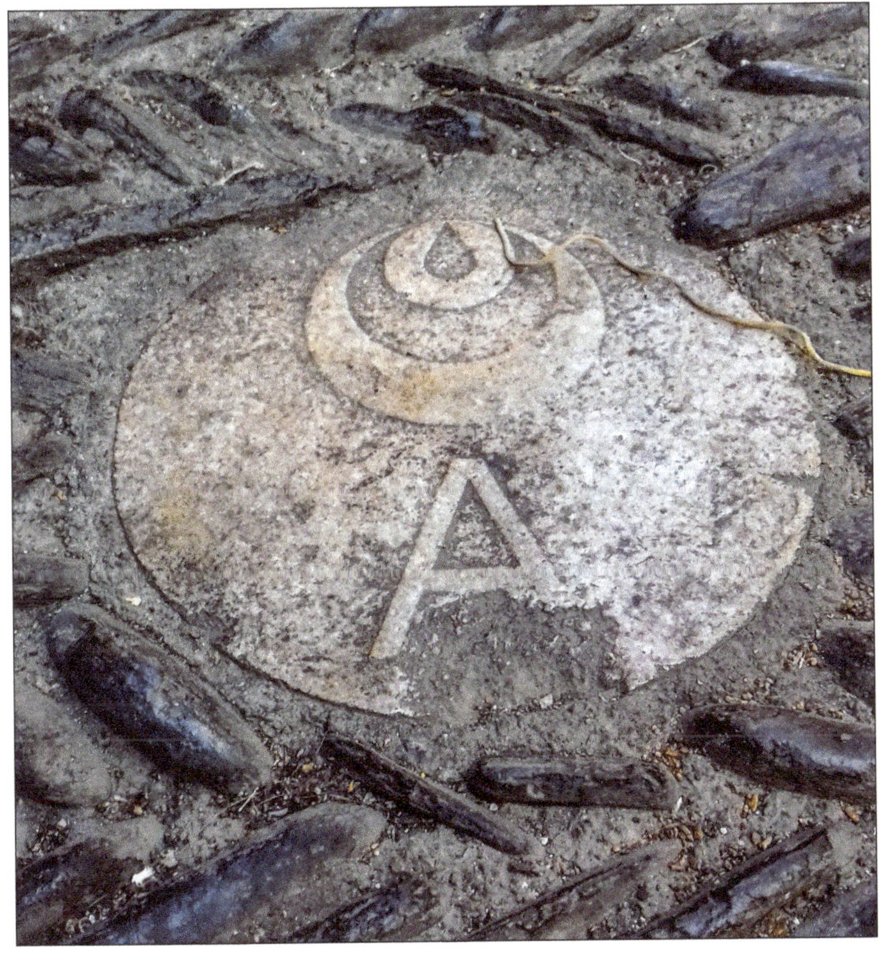
A

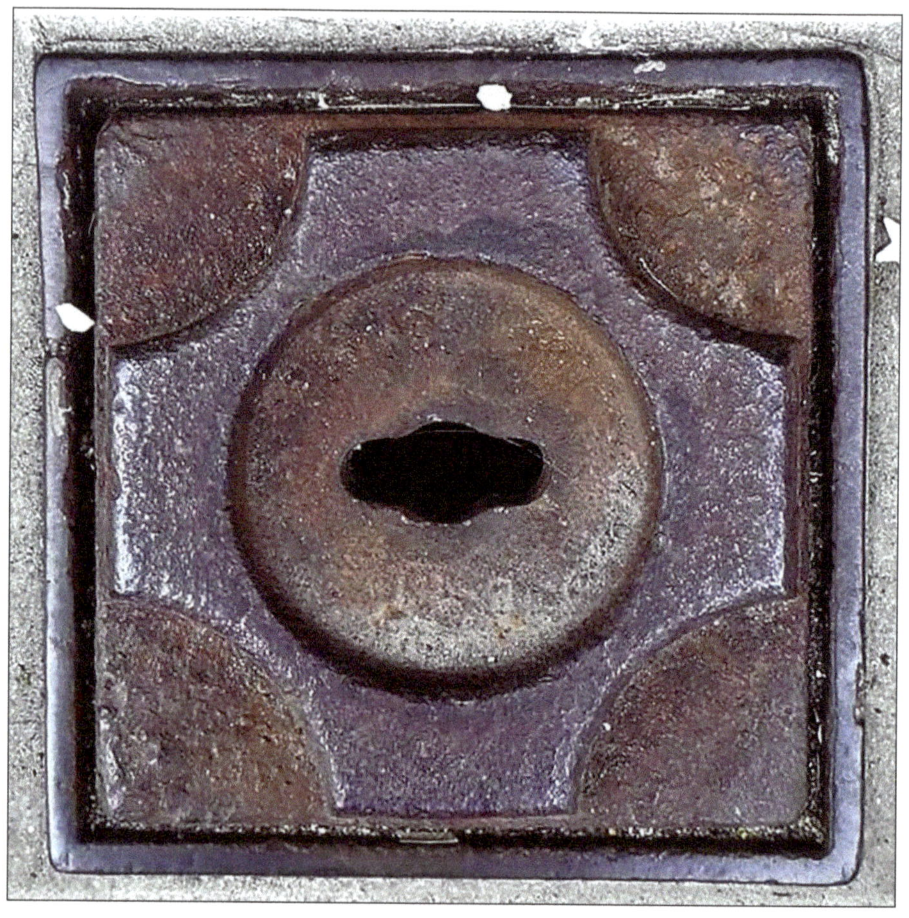

There is also the shocking incident of Jodie S Lane who was electrocuted whilst walking her pooch in New York after stepping on a metal manhole cover. This wasn't an isolated occurrence. You will be relieved to know that voltage emissions from manhole covers are now monitored.

There is a growing appreciation of manhole covers around the world. The Japanese have an annual convention that celebrates their designs and there are a number of books to keep Japanese drain spotters content.

Numerous Facebook groups exist that celebrate a mutual fondness for these wonderfully ubiquitous objects. One group delights in sharing spectacular or unusual finds but have rather interesting rules of engagement. For example, photographs have to include at least one shoe in the shot. The make of shoe is also required. The size helps to scale the object. I have no idea why the brand of shoe is needed , but it makes for an interesting and fun read. This particular Facebook group holds an AGM

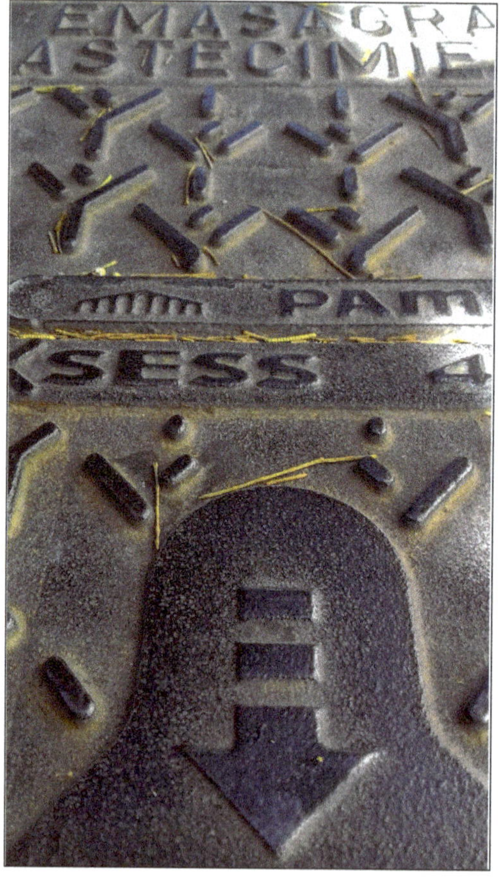

in Southport UK, with members attending from around the globe.

There are a plethora of people who have an interest in rubbing manholes. These enthusiasts have been observed, on their knees, frantically rubbing and waxing Thomas Crapper's manholes. This is to obtain an enduring memento of their visit to Westminster School in London. Mr Crapper (1836-1910) is famous for inventing the floating ballcock and founding the eponymous Thomas Crapper Sanitary Equipment Company in 1861. Hence going for a crap?

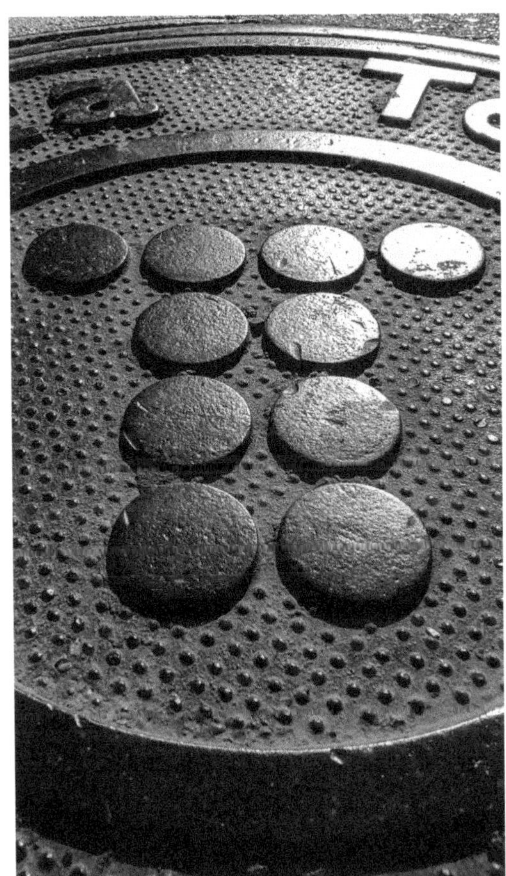

Artist Emma-France Raff has taken the concept of manhole rubbing a stage further. Emma is known for her inspirational t-shirt designs. A self-acclaimed manhole pirate, she and her father were inspired by the manholes they discovered on the streets of Alentejo in Portugal. Emma moved to Berlin in 2008 and formed her printmaking project called Raubdruckerin, inspired by the manhole covers that form a footprint of Berlin. Raubdruckerin is based in Berlin but has out-posts in other cities including Amsterdam, Lisbon and Paris. This innovative concept has elevated street art from ground level to chest height, taking the well-trodden yet mainly unnoticed designs to a wider audience.

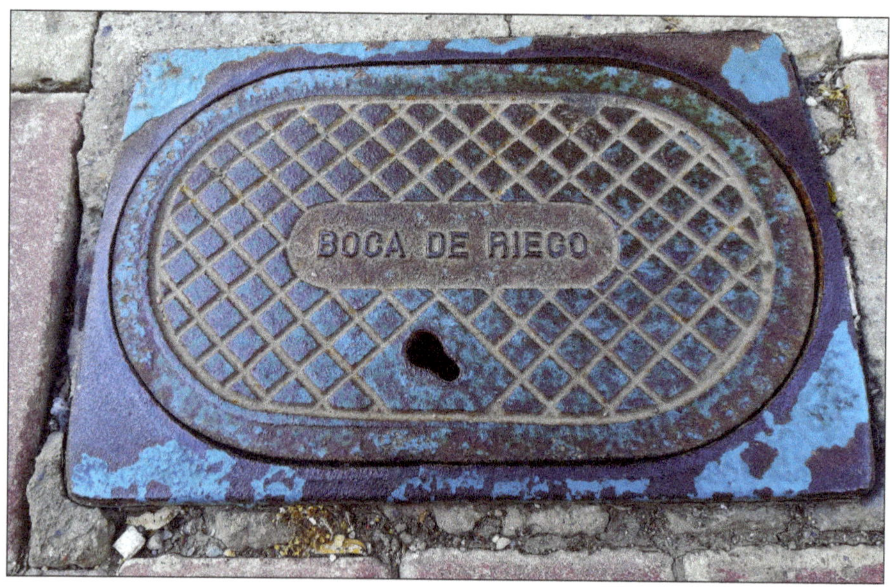

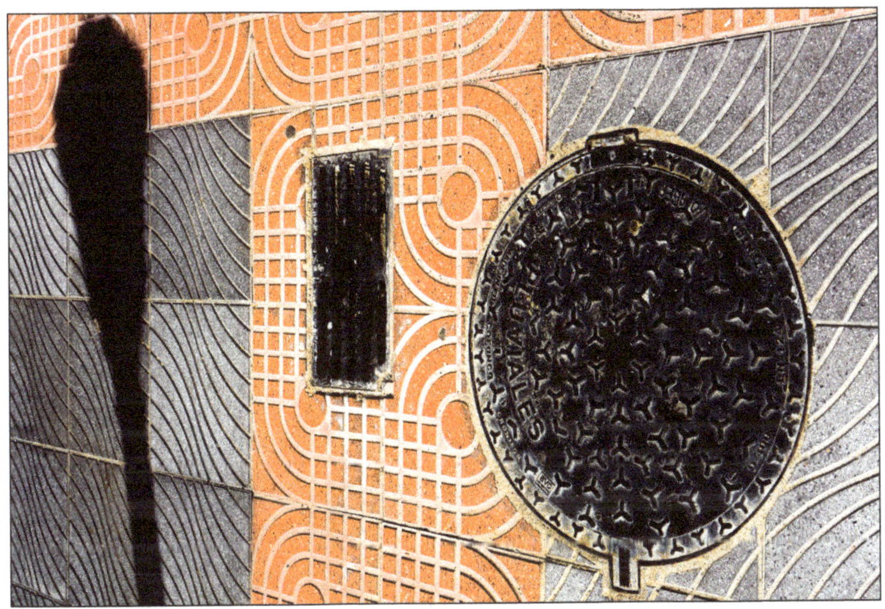

Drainspotters are growing in number throughout the world. The Japanese have even introduced collectable manhole cards. These are awarded when manhole enthusiasts seek out prized examples throughout their cities and towns.

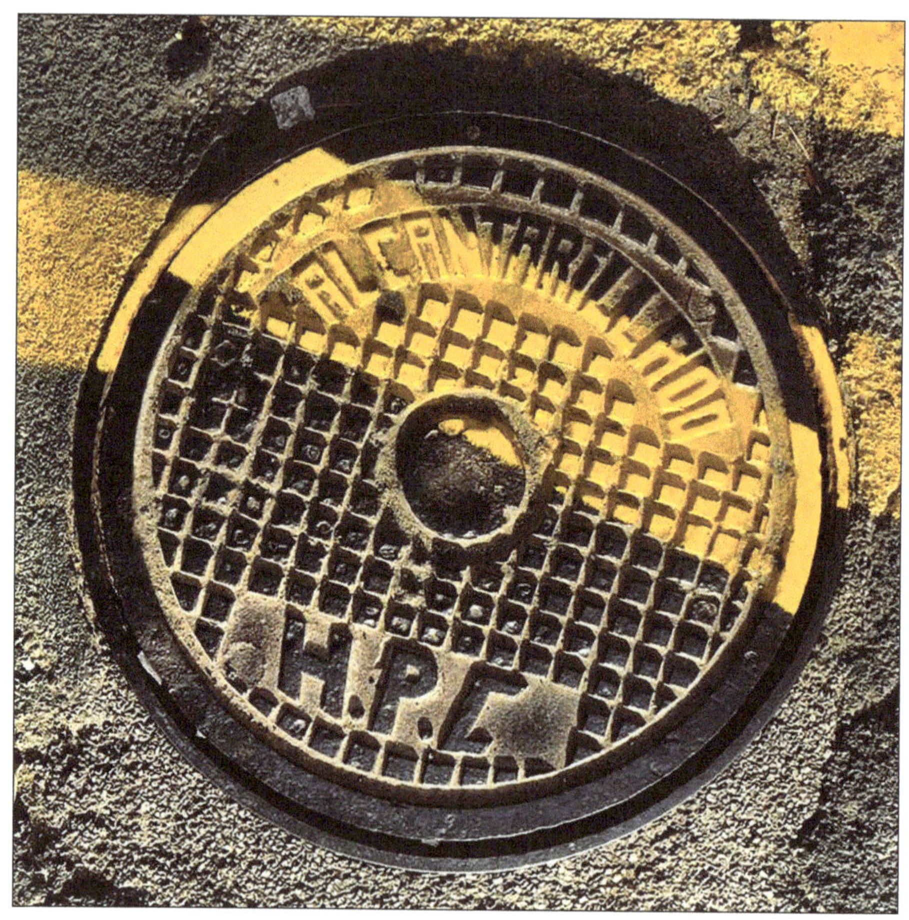
H.P.Z

The manhole rubbers photographers, t-shirt designers and Facebook groups are all helping to put manholes on the artistic map of the world. There are even a couple of horror movies that involve manholes, notably for the Japanese market. How they compare to the splendid Carol Reed film *The Third Man*, which also features manholes, and starring Orson Welles, I will let readers decide.

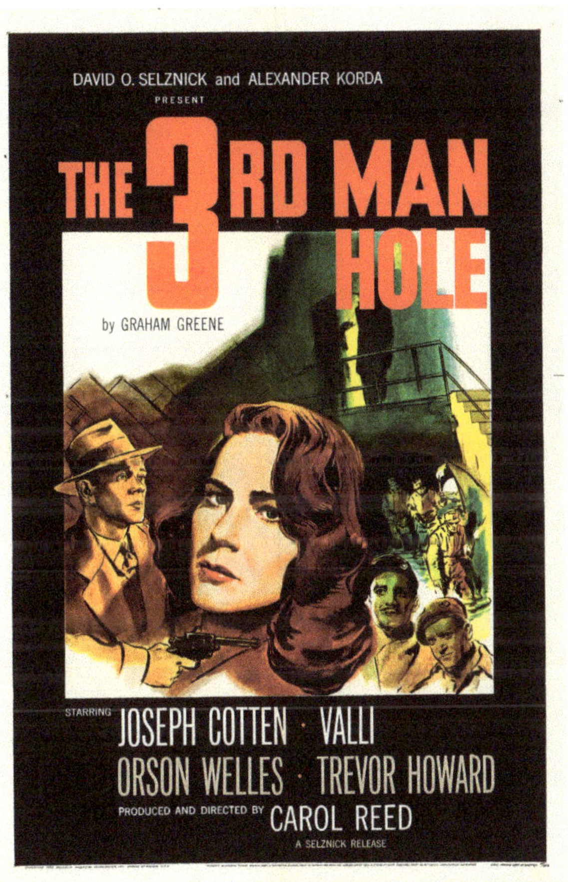

PD-Art (PD-US-not renewed)

There are also a number of short documentaries that can be found on the internet that focus on the manufacturing process of manholes.

One film provides an insight into the foundry that provides manhole covers for the sewers in New York.

Film maker and enthusiast Natasha Raheja, has made a fascinating documentary entitled *Cast in India*. Raheja's film took her to Howrah, near the Bay of Bengal, where the foundry is located. It is shocking to witness the appalling working conditions that the poorly waged workers have to endure. The film shows half- naked men working in the extreme heat of the foundry with scant regard for health and safety. These men risk their lives and health in a foundry that supplies New York, one of the world's richest cities with sewer covers. This is in stark comparison to conditions evidenced with Nagashima Imono Casting Factory in Japan. Oona McGee, writer and editor, made a short documentary that celebrates the prolific Japanese manhole industry. High tech processes are in place and workers operate in conditions safe and appropriate for the 21st century manufacturing sector.

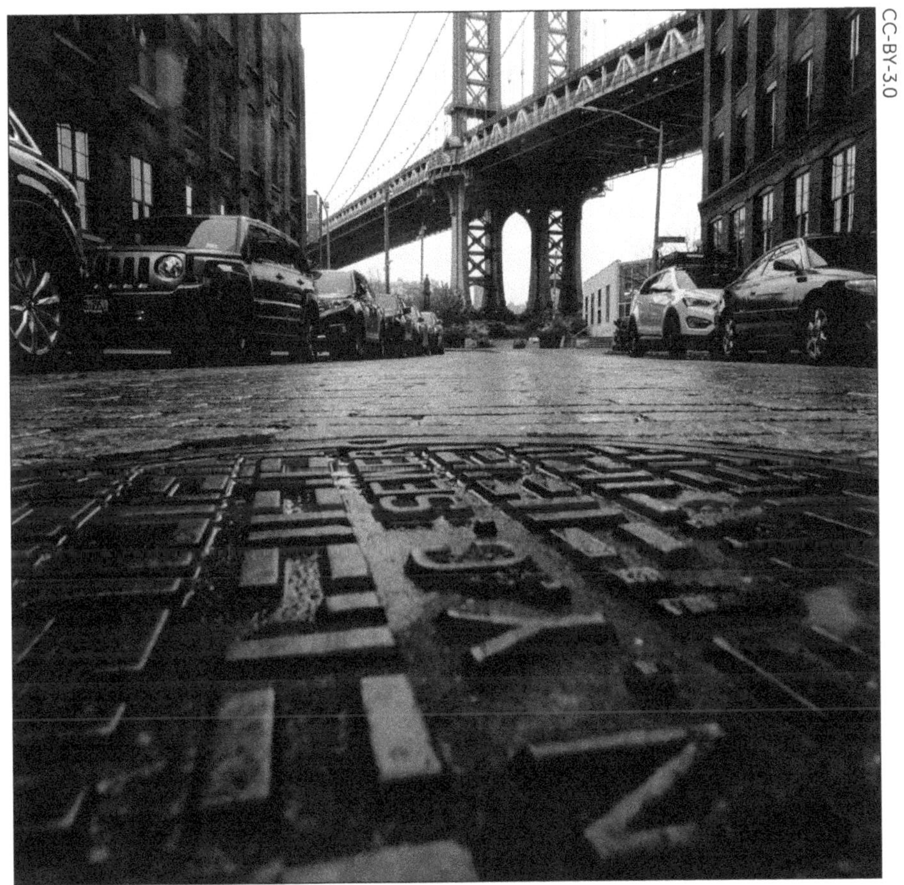

Dumbo, Brooklyn Worm's-eye view

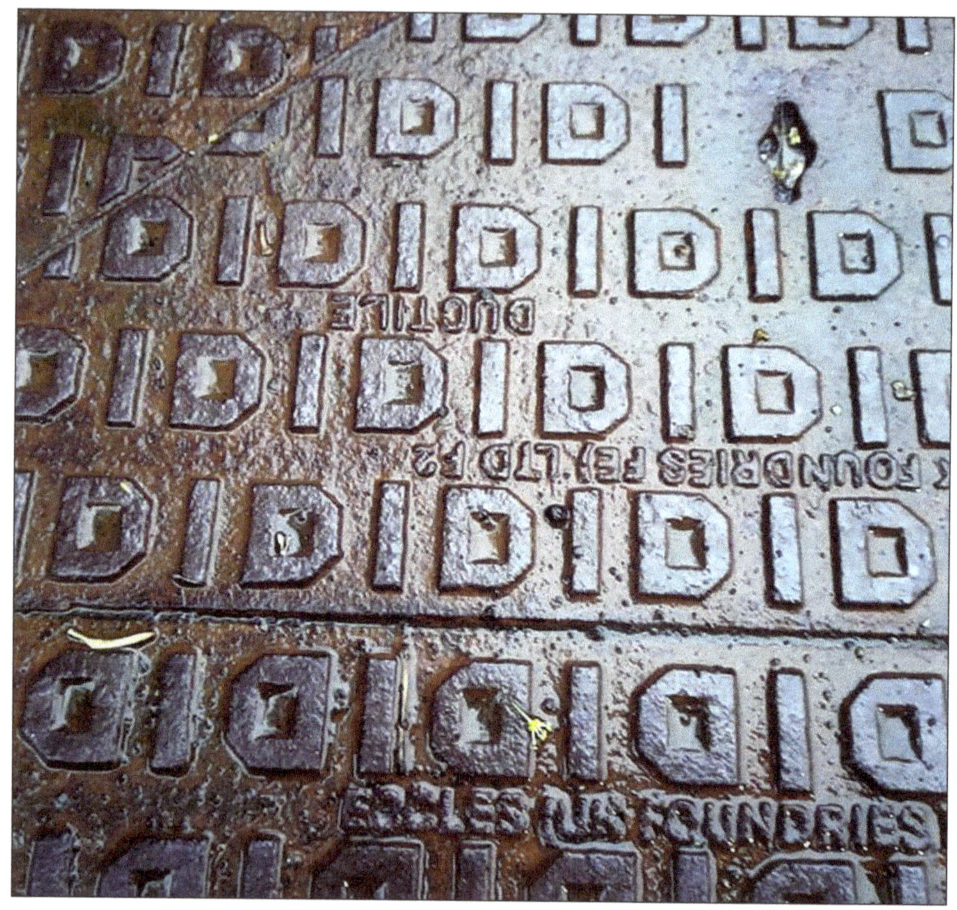
DUCTILE
FOUNDRIES

In conclusion

The appreciation of manhole design and manufacture is definitely on the rise. I am delighted. My ambition to raise their profile through photography is no longer a lonely fetish as I once thought. I am thrilled that so many drainspotters around the world are helping to promote their prominence.

Whether they are photographers, t-shirt designers, rubbers, manhole designers, film makers or just fanatics or thieves, I am over the moon.

From my initial concept I wondered if this art form had a name. I could not find one. Instead I decided to invent a name for this genre.

HEAVY METAL

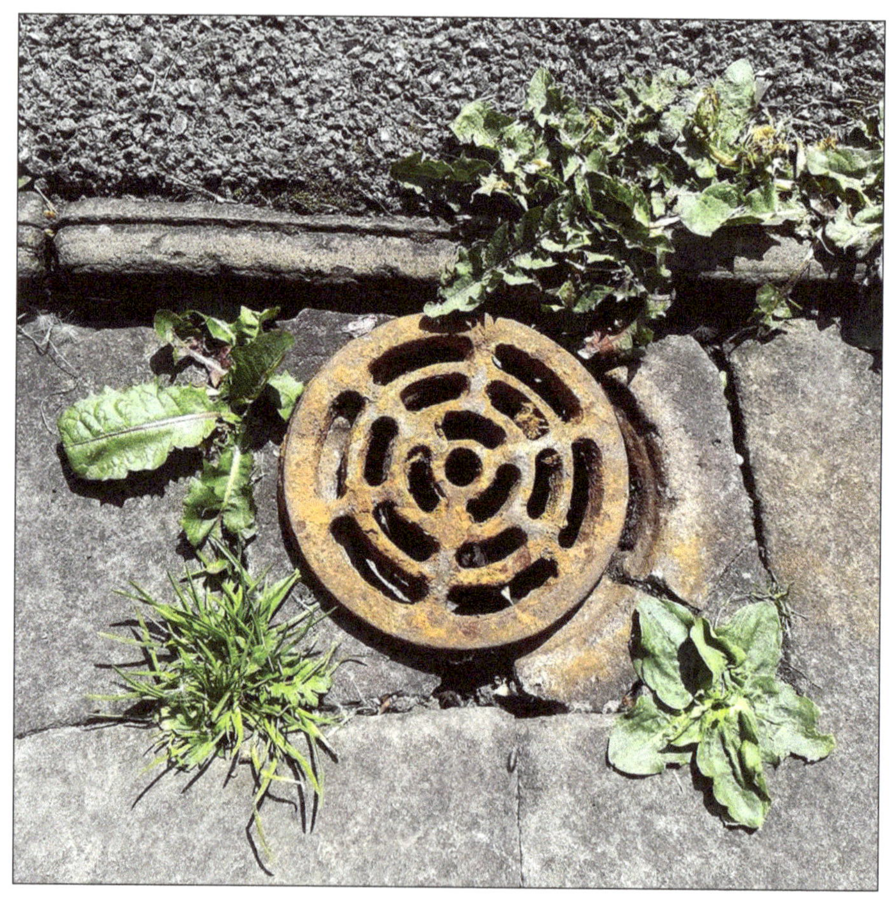

My genre of manhole photography and related art forms was born on the day of my first exhibition in 2017, **FunkistKunst**. I think it embodies industrial street architecture photography and hope that this continues to grow globally. You can view the website at www.funkistkunst.com

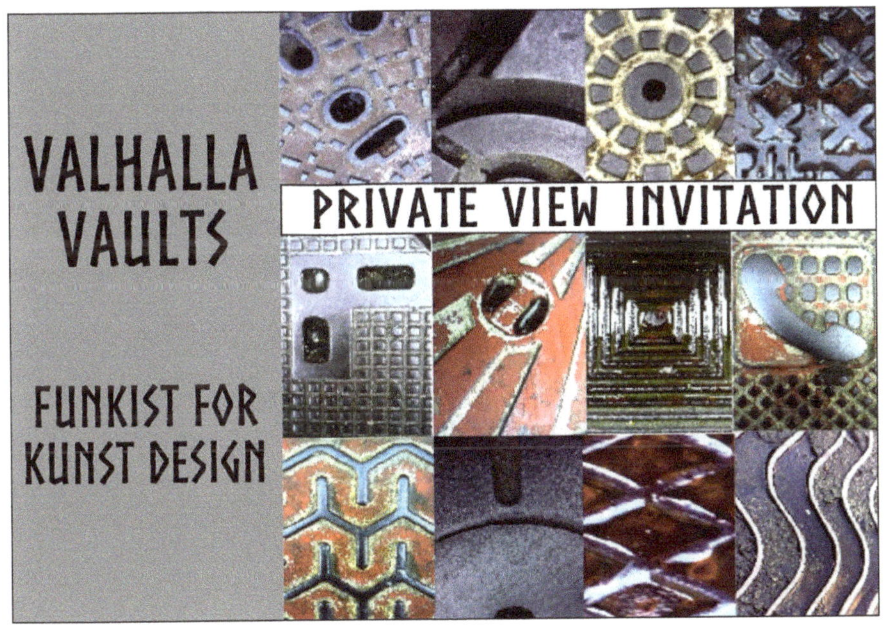

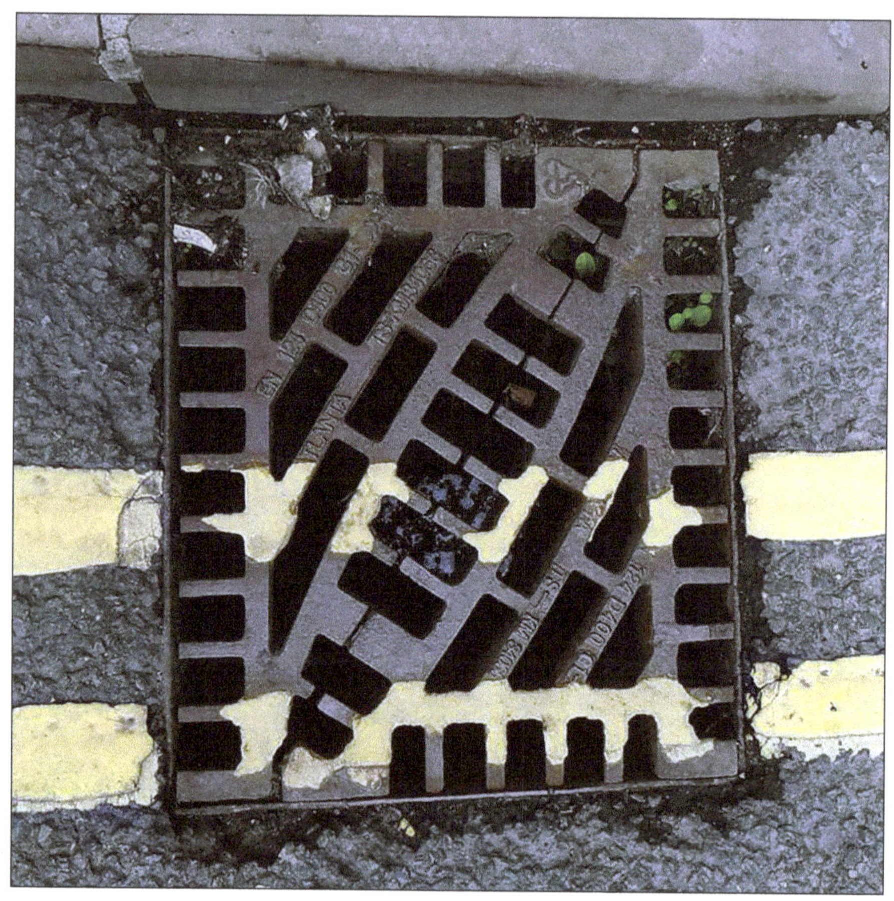

I wish you all fabulous adventures finding manholes in the future.

I will be seeking out new holes and civilisations on the ground in South America and the Far East.

Happy hunting Drainspotters and gridders.

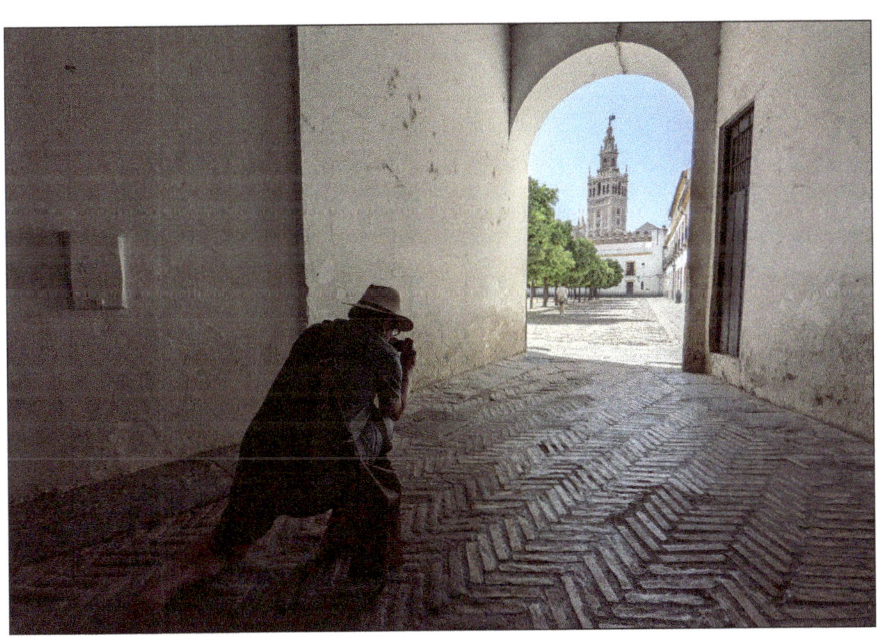

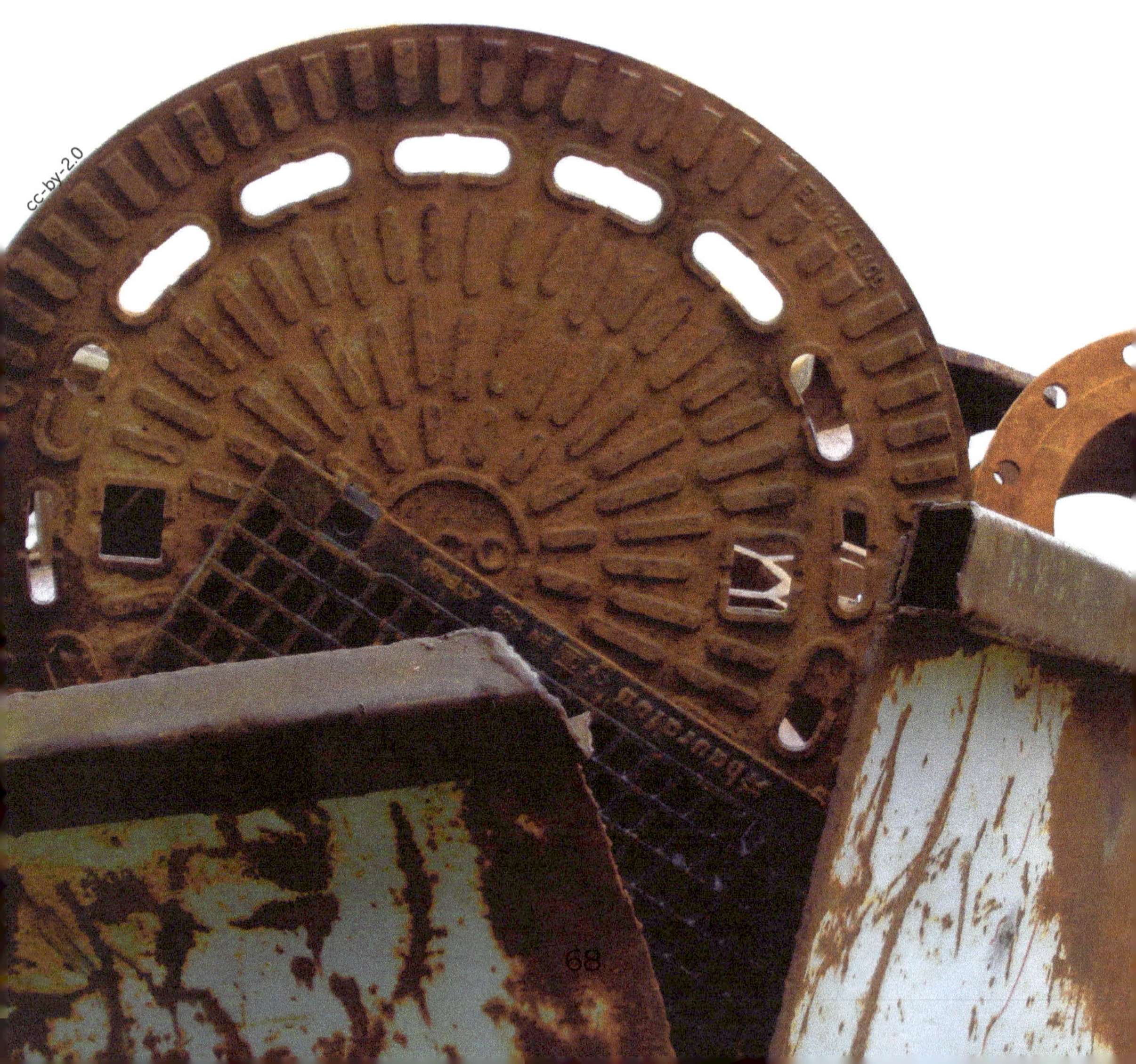

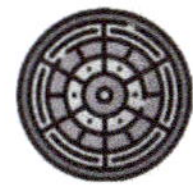

Photo References

IV: **Hayward** St Leonards-on-Sea, Sussex UK 2018. Taken close to The Royal Victoria Hotel where princess Victoria stayed in 1834.

VI: left **Gafas de sol** Málaga, southern Spain 2017. An unusual and quirky hole that made me smile.

VI: Right **Drain in Spain**, Salobrena 2017. The azul sky reflected in the water below the grid, a reminder of a scorchio day.

X: I came across this image in Motril, a working town on the southern coast of Spain 2018. I liked the manhole in the foreground with the wheels in shot.

XII: **Oro** Discovered Granada 2018. An opulent cover that evoked images of Spain at the height of its riches. The

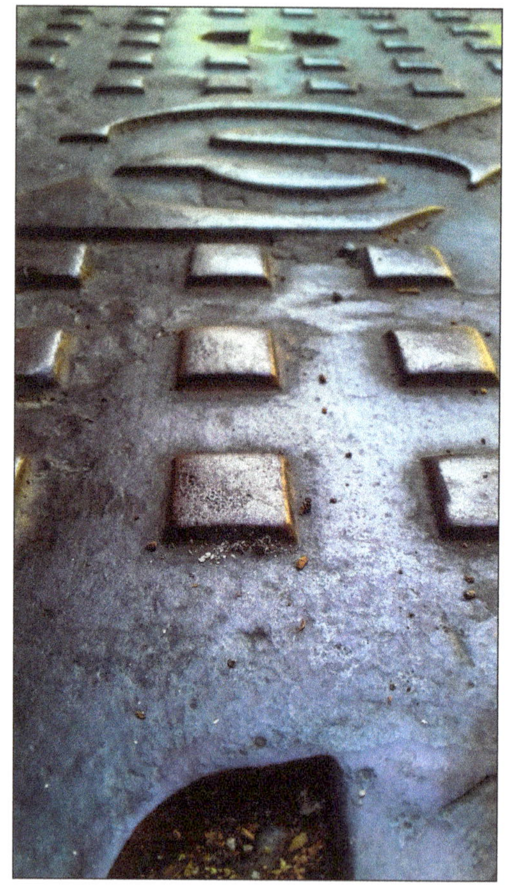

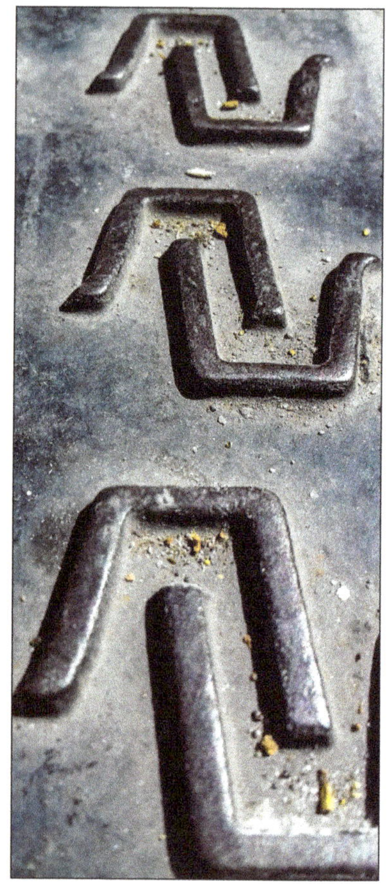

metal work casting is impressive. The light and shade intrigued my eye.

XIV: **Emasesa** Seville Spain 2018. I like the variety of colours displayed together alongside the nifty nodules.

Page 2: **ONO Not Again** Seville, Spain 2018. I love this funky chunky hole.

Page 4: **Blue Flame** Granada, Spain 2018.

Page 5: **ALPU** Malaga, Spain 2018.

Page 6: **Mellalergy** Glossop, UK 2020.

Page 7: **Insane drain** Seville, Spain 2020.

Page 8: **Scream Unawatuna**, Sri Lanka, 2020. Discovered in a hotel garden beside a swimming pool. The rusted metal work reminded of a screaming mouth.

Page 10: First manhole exhibition in Cardiff, Wales 2017. Opening night, photo courtesy of Alan Bloomfield.

Page 11: **Exhibition poster** 2017.

Page 12: Images from first exhibition 2017.

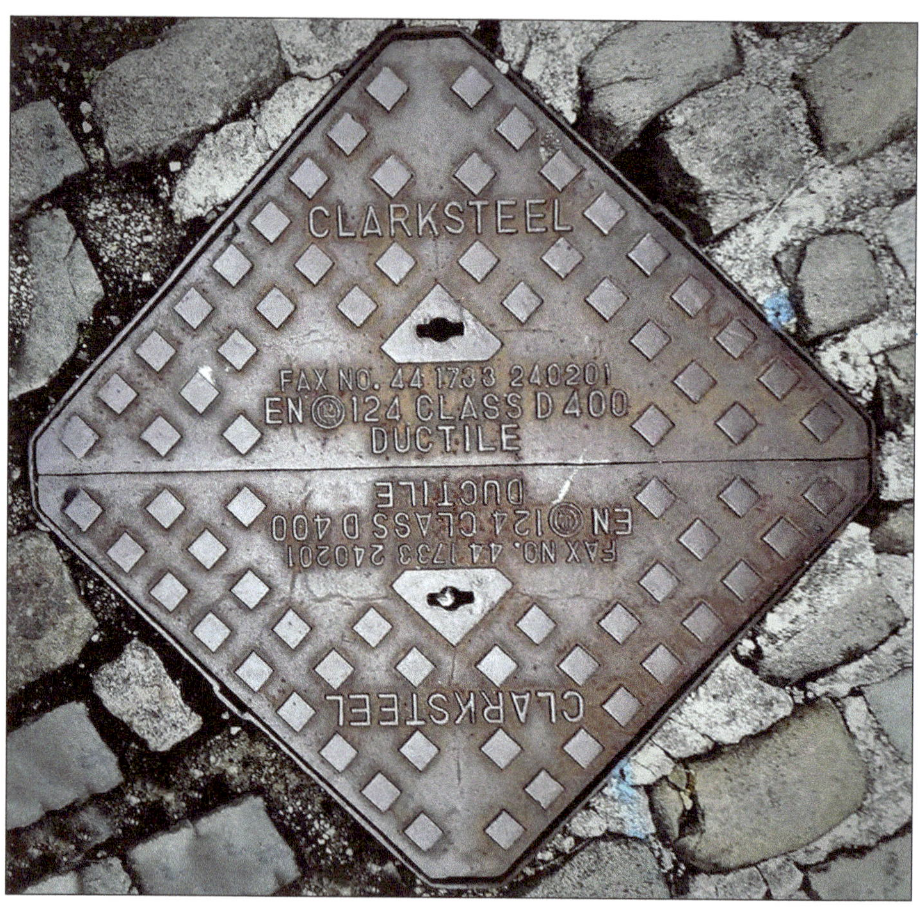
CLARKSTEEL
FAX NO. 44 1733 240201
EN 124 CLASS D 400
DUCTILE

Page 13: Exhibition photo featuring Bryan Robert Bale delivering the opening speech, courtesy of Alan Bloomfield.

Page 14: Left image **Hose pipes** Seville, Spain 2018.

Page 14: Right image **Dial M** image from exhibition 2017.

Page 16: Tryptic set in stone processed photos images from Spain and manchester 2018

Page 17: Tryptic set in stone processed photos images from Spain and manchester 2018.

Page 19: Seville, Spain 2018 I enjoyed the artistry of the painted bricks and manhole.

Page 20: Amusing little number from Guajar Faraguit, Spain 2018.

Page 21: **Chameleon Supercable** Almunecar, Spain 2018.
Page 22: **Sandblasted** Motril, Spain 2018.

Page 23: **Valsu** Motril, Spain 2018.

Page 24: **ICT** Malaga Spain 2018.

Page 25: Tryptic processed holes set in stone, somewhere in Spain 2018.

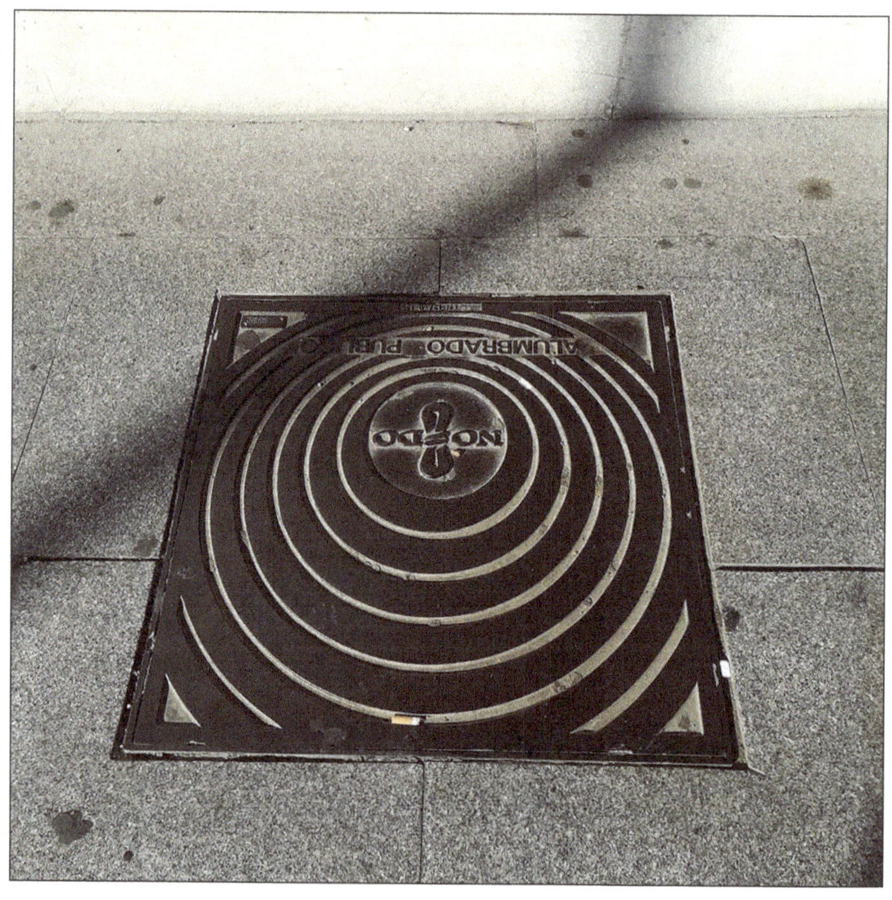
ALUMBRADO

Page 27: **E Square** Salobrena, Spain 2018. The composition amused me.

Page 28: **Squirty Hole** Broadbottom, Greater Manchester 2019. This hole tickled me, nothing more.

Page 30: A rare opportunity, a photo taken because of the blue sky reflected in the murky water beneath the grid,Granada, Spain 2017. No processing required,a lucky fluke?

Page 31: **A fishy number**, Copenhagen if I recall 2018.

Page 32: Photo courtesy of Sue Densley on her trip to Matsuyama, Japan 2018.

Page 34: Three heavy metal holes from Spain 2018. Right image is from Granada and denotes the emblem of the city, a pomegranate.

Page 35: **Sundial** from Unawatuna, Sri Lanka 2020.

Page 43: Tryptic Torrox, Spain 2018.

Page 46: Verdant hole from space. St Leonards, UK 2018.

Page 48: **Zig Zogg** Malaga, Spain 2017 courtesy of Alan Bloomfield.

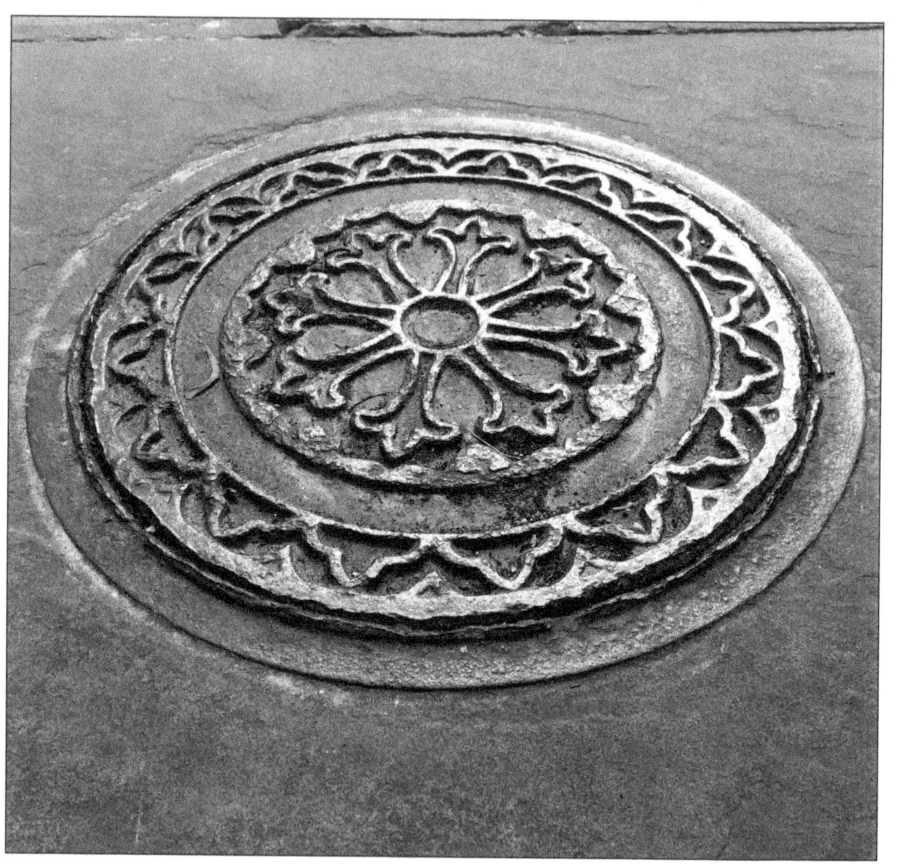

Page 49: Left image **Ominous look** Manchester, UK 2021.

Page 49: Right image a rusted hole in a forgotten location and dateline.

Page 50: **Nasa?** Madrid, Spain 2021.

Page 51: **An old flame** Madrid, Spain 2021.

Page 52: **A Key Stone** place forgotten circa 2021.

Page 54: **Pam says 4!** Madrid, Spain 2019.

Page 55: **Duro Dinero** Madrid, Spain 2019.

Page 56: **Blue Mouth** Nerja, Spain 2019.

Page 57: **ET is watching you!** Salobrena, Spain 2017 courtesy of Alan Bloomfield.

Page 58: **Anarchic Hole** I just love the disruption. Spain 2018.

Page 62: **Ken Dodd died today! Diddi?**. Broadbottom station, Greater Manchester, UK 2019.

Page 64: **Greenery** St Leonards, Sussex, UK 2018.

Page 65: **First exhibition poster** 2017.

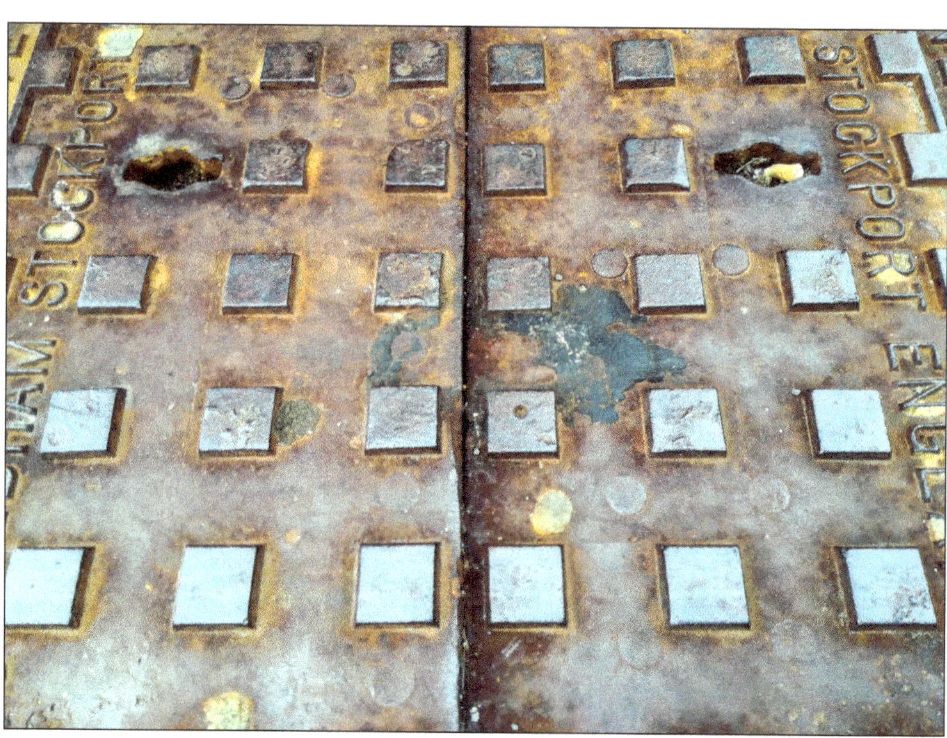
STOCKPORT
STOCKPORT
STOCKPORT

Page 66: Glossop, UK 2020.

Page 67: Author in action Seville, Spain 2020 courtesy of Steve Talbot.

Page 70: Left image **Space Command** Madrid , Spain 2021
Right image: **Jiggy** Madrid, Spain 2021

Page 72: **Stoned Steel** Manchester Science Museum 2019, this can be found in the impressive goods yard within the museum. The goods yard was part of the Liverpool Road Station, the Manchester terminus of the Liverpool and Manchester Railway and the first purpose-built passenger railway.

Page 74: **Waved Metal** Seville, Spain 2018

Page 76: **Regal Iron** St Leonards-on-Sea, Sussex UK 2018.

Page 78: **Formidable Doors** Manchester UK 2020

www.ingramcontent.com/pod-product-compliance
Ingram Content Group UK Ltd.
Pitfield, Milton Keynes, MK11 3LW, UK
UKHW061949290726
14090UKWH00021B/1144

9 781913 898496